Navigating the Winds of Change

NAVIGATING THE WINDS OF CHANGE

Staying on Course in Business & in Life

Andy Kaufman

INSTITUTE FOR LEADERSHIP EXCELLENCE AND DEVELOPMENT

Navigating the Winds of Change

Copyright ©2002 by Andy Kaufman

Published by Zurich Press

Cover design: Cindy Kiple

First printing 2002

ISBN 0-9720587-0-2

Printed in the United States of America

15	14	13	12	11	10	09	08	07	06	05	04	03	02
12	11	10	9	8	7	6	5	4	3	2	1		

To Sara,
The exclamation point
of my life

Contents

▼

Introduction

▼

"CHANGE IS THE ONLY CONSTANT!"

THAT STATEMENT MADE more than 2,500 years ago by an ancient philosopher certainly holds true today! The winds of change have challenged mankind throughout the ages. In just the past 150 years, think how radical the introductions of electricity, telephones, automobiles, and radio were to their particular time periods! In some ways, the challenges of change are nothing new, but the study of how we have navigated change over the years can help us today.

However, as our new century unfolds, there are reasons to believe we are experiencing unprecedented conditions, as the chart below indicates. The winds are seemingly blasting from all directions. *Change-storms* are more frequent and frontal systems less predictable than before. Basic support structures that helped us weather—even harness—previous changes are less firmly grounded.

Change comes from all directions—technology, global economy, socio-political. Change today is more frequent and less predictable.

TIME LAPSE BETWEEN IDEA AND MASS PRODUCTION

800 years	**STEAM ENGINE** (988-1788)
112	**PHOTOGRAPHY** (1727-1839)
56	**TELEPHONE** (1820-1876)
35	**RADIO** (1867-1902)
3	**INTEGRATED CIRCUIT** (1958-1961)
0.9	**NETSCAPE** (1994; Feb.–Dec.)

The gap in time between an idea and its introduction into mass production is growing shorter and shorter.

Almost regardless of the industry we work in, we have personally experienced the powerful winds of change. The hurricane force of technological change has ravaged entire companies and product lines practically overnight, while providing extraordinary opportunity for people who could take advantage of the conditions. As leaders in our companies, we have found ourselves faced with needing new skills, new ways of doing things— even new ways of explaining the world around us. If this time of high change was only a temporary blip on the radar screen, perhaps we could just head below and weather out the storm. But the reality is that rapid change and uncertainty are here to stay.

Learning how to effectively manage change is one of the fundamental skills we must develop to be excellent leaders.

Though we might intellectually acknowledge this truth, many of the people I have talked with in corporate America have not felt an urgent need to improve their change-management skills. It could be a general, prevailing sense that we are all getting along sufficiently. It could also be that much of the writing and training on the topic has been heavy on theory and cliché and light on practical tools. Regardless, that all changed after the tragic terrorist attacks of September 11, 2001, and the events that followed. Suddenly our entire nation was face-to-face with the reality that things are now different, and we need skills to help us through the transition. As MSNBC correspondent Jill Nelson reported on October 15, 2001, "Normal doesn't exist anymore." As we all face the prospects of a new world, it is clear that learning how to effectively manage change is now a high priority. It is my firm conviction that this is one of the fundamental skills we must develop to be excellent leaders. Thus, it is critical that we begin to consider ourselves students of change—striving to understand the dynamics that change introduces—and to continually enhance our ability to not just survive but to increasingly become comfortable in an ever-fluctuating and uncertain environment.

THE SCOPE OF THIS BOOK

This book focuses on two particular aspects of managing change. The first is how to deal with change on a personal basis—tools for keeping pace with the dizzying flurry of transitions in your life. The second is how to manage change in your organization—tools to help you more effectively lead change when you step back into the windstorms after reading this book.

Certainly, there are those who God created to be more change-hardy than others. Good for you if you happen to be one of them! Let me be clear: I was not wired that way! This realization led to years of research on the topic to better enable me and those I was responsible to lead to be effective in an environment of ambiguity. Through this journey, I have uncovered fundamental lessons and concepts that can help us all learn to more effectively manage change, regardless of how we were wired.

This book contains more content than can typically be covered in the keynote presentations and workshops I present to organizations around the country. My goal is to boil down the oceans of information on this vital topic into a concise, readable book that addresses what I consider essential for successfully navigating the winds of change. This book is not about what works in theory or on a whiteboard! This material has been proven in the day-to-day changes and windstorms of my life and the lives of those I have had the privilege to sail with thus far. This information has been crucial to helping many stay on course, and I am excited to share it with you.

WHY USE A SAILING METAPHOR?

In the mid-1980s, I developed an interest in sailing. Though by just about any definition I am simply a *hack* sailor, I have always found sailing to be an engaging recreation. There are many aspects of sailing that model issues we face in real life, not the least of which is how change factors into a sailor's journey. Though no metaphor is perfect, I have found the use of word pictures to be helpful in my learning and teaching experience, and I trust this one will be helpful to yours, regardless of whether or not you have stepped foot on a sailboat.

YOUR MISSION

To get the most value from this book, I want to challenge you to do the following:

- Actively engage in the reading of this book! Pull out a pen or a highlighter. Mark up the pages, noting where ideas apply to your life and where you want to learn more. Don't let these words just drift off into the bin of "interesting reading" without allowing them to influence changes you are currently experiencing.

- Identify at least one lesson, tool, or tip that you can take away from here and actually put to use right away. You will likely find more than one application, but do find at least one that you can and will directly apply to your life.

- Take the information from this book, along with your notes and personal insight, and pass it on to someone in your area of influence. Talk to someone about it! Talk about what you agree with, and even what you might not! Perhaps this is the gift you need to give to a person who is striving to be a better leader. Whether it be colleagues at work, or friends, or family at home, sharing this information will have the additional benefit of further sealing it in your life (not to mention benefiting the people in your circle as well).

Checking the
Wind Conditions

▼

CHANGE IS A MAJOR THEME just about anywhere you look. Think about it the next time you glance at the headlines in a newspaper, magazine, or trade journal. I happen to have a recent issue of *Investor's Business Daily* in front of me. The feature articles include stories about the impact of a surprising jump in the core Consumer Price Index, how to manage a business when margins are down, and warnings about avoiding stocks with certain price patterns. All of these are a response to the winds of change. Each seeks to provide perspective on how to keep your portfolio on course.

Once you learn to be more comfortable in a fluctuating environment, there is no limit to where you can go.

See how the themes and challenges of change—which we will be discussing throughout this book—jump out at you when you watch someone you dearly care for go through a difficult illness, or you talk with a friend who has just been laid off. When the next frontal system hits your life, observe how your reactions correspond to the principles of change. Once you learn to see the world through the eyes of change, there is no going back. On the other hand, once you learn to be more comfortable in a fluctuating environment, there is no limit to where you can go.

PERSONAL CHANGE INVENTORY

How much have you been affected by the winds of change? It could be you have gone through more transitions lately than you even realize. Take a few minutes to review the following lists. Check off each item that is true or mostly true about you in the last two years.

Work/Career

- [ ] Have a new employer
- [ ] Working from home more often
- [ ] Are doing the same or more with fewer people
- [ ] Are/were worried about losing job
- [ ] Significant change in revenue and/or earnings outlook
- [ ] Using a wireless device for communication
- [ ] Spending more time in meetings
- [ ] Increasing need to be face-to-face with customers
- [ ] Have more to read and seemingly less time to do it
- [ ] Receive cell phone calls during non-work hours
- [ ] Using more consultants or temporary workers than before
- [ ] Have one (or more) new supervisors/managers
- [ ] Using or considering the use of a coach/mentor
- [ ] Increased ability to relate to a character in *Dilbert!*
- [ ] Job impact due to social or political unrest
- [ ] Greater emphasis on global marketplace
- [ ] Have part (or all) of your systems work outsourced
- [ ] Are (or became) a "consultant"
- [ ] Have been promoted
- [ ] Became more proficient with a software package
- [ ] Experienced job termination
- [ ] Organization was merged, acquired, or reorganized
- [ ] Worked for an employer who went out of business
- [ ] Started own business
- [ ] Changed to a new type of work
- [ ] Changed work hours
- [ ] Changed work dress code
- [ ] Learned a new methodology/process
- [ ] Terminated at least one employee
- [ ] Experienced pressure to deliver work more quickly
- [ ] Started using a new operating system (e.g. Linux)
- [ ] Experienced greater emphasis on teams and empowerment

Personal

- ☐ Got married
- ☐ Got divorced
- ☐ Welcomed a new family member (birth/adoption/live-in relative)
- ☐ Had a major purchase or mortgage
- ☐ Moved at least once
- ☐ Suffered the death of a spouse or close family member
- ☐ Suffered the death of a close friend
- ☐ Experienced serious illness, disability, or diagnosis
- ☐ Experienced a change in personal finances (good or bad)
- ☐ Took a vacation
- ☐ Started a new hobby, sport, or recreation
- ☐ Started/increased emphasis on planning for retirement
- ☐ Changed religious beliefs
- ☐ Changed political beliefs
- ☐ Knew someone affected by violence or crime
- ☐ Increased anxiety about personal safety
- ☐ Had a spouse start or stop working
- ☐ Spending less time reading newspapers
- ☐ Have two or more phone lines at home
- ☐ Buying more on the Internet
- ☐ Trading stocks electronically
- ☐ Increasingly using a PDA (e.g. Palm, PocketPC)

After checking off item after item, hopefully you have an increased appreciation for all the change you have encountered lately. Was every circumstance painful? Some, perhaps, but certainly not all.

We often consider change something negative that is inflicted upon us. However, both negative and positive transitions affect our lives.

From the lists above, you see that many of the changes could be considered positive *or* negative. Yet in the context of *managing change*, we often consider change to be something negative that is inflicted upon us. However, it is important to realize that both negative and positive transitions affect our lives. We will discuss this in greater detail later.

To finalize this exercise of checking the wind conditions, please take a moment to reflect on your current situation. How would you summarize the top 3-5 changes you are dealing with right now? Think about this and then write down your responses in the area below.

TOP 3-5 CHANGES IN MY PERSONAL AND PROFESSIONAL LIFE RIGHT NOW

_____

_____

_____

_____

_____

As we discuss various principles of change in this book, keep these primary transitions in mind. Ask yourself how each principle relates to your situation. Does your experience agree with what is being communicated? Is there an aspect of the discussion that you can start applying immediately to help you through your changes? By keeping your current challenges in sight, you can more effectively apply the lessons you are about to learn.

CHAPTER TWO

The Dynamics of Change

▼

THERE SEEMS TO BE no shortage of books, classes, and seminars on the topic of dealing with change. Yet my observation is that the dynamics of change are poorly understood, highly resisted, and all too often just ignored. Though we encounter change on a daily basis, our formal training over the years has left us essentially unprepared for our task of managing the changes we face today. When seeking advice, we often hear conflicting opinions or simple clichés. For example, here are a few types of counsel I've come across recently:

"If it ain't broke, break it!"
"When it is not necessary to change, it is necessary not to change."[1]
"Embrace change!"
"Be a change agent!"
"That's the way it is. Deal with it!"
"Just follow these ten easy steps . . . ."

Change is a process, not an event or a destination. It is a process that cannot be trivialized into easy tips, checklists, or one-size-fits-all solutions. Change, by definition, will never be mastered because each situation is unique and we each respond in unique ways. Even similar changes can yield radically different results! For example, one person can lose their job and yet end up in a situation they completely love. They actually feel thankful the change occurred. Another person could encounter the same circumstance and start a downward spiral, like the man I heard of recently whose job loss led to a divorce, forfeiting custody of his children, and such poor health that he could not drive. Fortunately, we can study the process of change and understand the dynamics involved with it, thus helping to harness the winds to our benefit.

Our formal training has left us essentially unprepared for our task of managing the changes we face today.

There is an interesting tension involved with change. On the one hand, we vigorously resist it as if our lives depended on it. There is perceived safety in stability, and we protect that cautiously. Yet at the same time, we have an essential, desperate need for change—so much so that our very lives *do* depend on it! I doubt any of us would sign up for a repetitious life like the one so humorously depicted in the movie *Groundhog Day*! Yet, just as a sailboat requires wind to sail, we were created to require change to survive.

So, we have this constant tension—this core dilemma—within us: the need to change, yet the desire for stability. Is there hope for those who are being thrown off course by the relentless winds and pounding waves? You bet there is! Let's use the sailing metaphor to cruise through some principles for navigating the winds of change!

PART 1

NAVIGATING
PERSONAL CHANGE

▼

AS WE CONSIDER THE TOPIC of managing personal change, here is how I am applying the sailing metaphor:

You are the *skipper*, the one at the helm, and the sole person responsible for sailing your boat. There is a sense in which you are the *boat* in my application of the metaphor as well.

The *crew* on your boat represents people in your life—people who are in your areas of influence. These can be family members, associates at work, neighbors, and friends. You could also consider these same people to be other *boats* or *boat captains* in the sea around you.

The *journey* in this metaphor represents your life.

The *destination* and *horizon* represent your long-term mission and objectives—where, and in a sense, why you are journeying at all.

The *winds, currents,* and *weather* symbolize changes that confront you on a daily basis—often uncontrollable, though perhaps able to be forecast to some degree.

Magnetic North and the *North Star* represent your personal values that remain changeless (or nearly changeless) throughout your journey.

The *rudder, sails,* and *instruments* are the tools you have at your disposal to interpret and respond to the winds and waves of change. Generally, these tools are things over which you have a high degree of control.

As you read through the principles of managing personal change, keep these definitions in mind and apply them accordingly.

I have divided the section on managing personal change into 13 areas. By understanding *and applying* these ideas, you will be well on your way to successfully learning to navigate the winds of personal change.

CHAPTER THREE

A Voyage Mindset

▼

IN MY PERSONAL STUDY of change I have read numerous books from many brilliant minds, I have reviewed scores of microfiche reels of old newspapers and trade journals to see how change was addressed historically, and I have analyzed my own life and observed the lives of many around me, including hundreds of coaching clients and workshop participants. In each case, my mission was to seek clues for how to most effectively respond to change. If I had to boil down everything I have learned about managing change into a single word, it would be this: *perspective.*

Webster's Dictionary calls *perspective* "the capacity to view things in their true relations or relative importance." When you get right down to it, isn't that really the issue when it comes to dealing with the winds and waves in your life—the ability to understand how they fit in relation to everything else going on?

> *If I had to boil down everything I have learned about managing change into a single word, it would be this:* perspective.

Earlier I mentioned headlines in a newspaper for investors. I subscribe to that paper specifically to help me understand how to interpret the effect of events on the performance of my investments. Does the price-index change mean I should consider buying or selling? Do any of my investments match a suspicious pattern that signals it is time to sell? Perhaps the primary reason we study the news is to help us gain the necessary perspective to respond productively.

I could save a lot of time writing—and you could save time reading—if it was as easy as saying, "Want to manage change well? Hey, just go get some perspective, pal!" Perspective is a good one-word answer for us. Learning how to gain perspective, though, is what the rest of this entire discussion is about.

THIS IS A JOURNEY

A great place to start with any skill development is to address how we think. I suggest you actively seek to develop what I call a *voyage mindset*. The voyage mindset requires us to realize that the journey is much bigger than any singular change, regardless of how major the change might seem. Have you experienced a job termination? Have the priorities in your organization veered in ways that do not benefit you? Have you been handed a new work assignment beyond your expertise? Have you been given responsibility for managing a challenging person? We need to widen our scope of vision—our perspective—to realize that each change is a leg in the entire life-long journey.

Even the changes which seem destined to capsize us are still just a leg in the overall journey of our lives.

Even the changes which seem destined to capsize us or throw us overboard are still just a leg in the overall journey of our lives. I recall being at the funeral of a young man who died in a car accident. Our hearts broke as we watched his wife and children walk to the front of the church. The pastor who spoke reassured us all that this young man was, indeed, in a better place since he had made peace with God many years earlier. The pastor then shared a perspective that took me by surprise at first, yet has proven to be true. In a loving way, he suggested that though this change was tragically difficult for the wife and kids right now, the years would show that the family would do more than just survive it. They would be surrounded by people who love them and who would help them through this, and over time they would live full lives marked, but not destroyed, by this event. In a sense, he was casting the perspective that even this tragedy—one that none of us would ever choose or wish for—is still only a leg in the overall journey.

It could be that you or someone you know has gone through a tragic change similar to this. I do not suggest that perspective is easy to attain (or maintain). However, there is power in actively seeking to develop this voyage mindset—in both the storms and the light winds—to help us through the leg we are sailing and to better enable us to stay on course.

THERE ARE NO ENDINGS?

As I recently browsed a magazine with all kinds of motivational posters and plaques, I saw one item with a beautiful sunrise peaking over a mountain range. The saying on the bottom reads:

There are no endings,
only beginnings.

Now I know what the creators were trying to get at, and I generally appreciate inspirational posters. However, I couldn't help but think that this one was blatantly *bad change doctrine!* When you think about it, isn't every new beginning by definition an ending as well?

Every time we encounter change in our lives, there is time required to *cope*, or respond, to the change. You get assigned a new boss? It takes time to understand what level of detail she wants, and if she prefers e-mail or voicemail. You get promoted with significant new responsibilities? It takes time to adjust to new team members, key stakeholders, and higher expectations. You get married? Even with armfuls of love, it takes time to get used to another person sharing your checkbook, your bathroom, and morning breath!

As humans, we are remarkably skilled at coping with change. The change/cope cycle is a part of our moment-to-moment existence. A gust of wind hits our sails, so we adjust our sails accordingly. In life as in sailing, such responses under typical circumstances usually occur without us even thinking about them.

THE FALL-BEHIND POINT

However, let's consider this cycle in the context of a high-change environment. A big wave hits, and as you adjust the rudder to compensate for it, another one crashes right behind it. While you are concentrating on the rolling waves, you realize the winds are gusting harder, and perhaps from a different direction. With experience, a good skipper handles this appropriately. But let's say this situation goes on for hours, or days. The mental intensity and the constant analysis and adjustment—not to mention the physical exhaustion from the turbulent seas—begin to take their toll. This scenario illustrates what a high-change environment is like for us. When we are unable to restore balance quickly enough to catch up with the most recent change, we hit what is called a *fall-behind point*.[2]

When one transition carries over to the next transition, and the next, you can be certain the fall-behind point is just around the corner.

Have you ever hit the fall-behind point? Individuals, teams, and organizations are all susceptible to it. The terrorist attacks of September 11, 2001, are a perfect example of even a nation hitting the fall-behind point. The first reports seemed to indicate a wayward plane—perhaps a Cessna or a corporate jet—crashing into the World Trade Center. Within minutes, and with cameras rolling, a second jet slammed into the other tower, and suddenly it was clear that this was not an accident. Just as the shock of New York City was starting to set in, news accounts reported smoke rising from the Pentagon in Washington, D.C., with another commercial jetliner being used as a guided missile. Within hours, reports of another hijacked plane heading toward Washington brought the country to a point of "Too much too quickly!" and made people ask, "What in the world is going on?"

Some people describe the fall-behind point as just being *numb,* or a feeling of *vertigo.* Others describe it as weeks of difficulty getting out of bed in the morning. When organizations reach the fall-behind point, their motto becomes "Whatever!" Many of the organizations my company helps are suffering from extended time beyond the fall-behind point and the resulting loss of productivity, morale, and income. When the baggage of trying to make one transition carries over to the next transition, which carries over to the next, you can be certain the fall-behind point is just around the corner.

NO CARRY-ONS!

So, what does the fall-behind point have to do with recognizing changes as endings? Glad you asked!

Our lives evidence our struggle to bring things to closure. You may have learned the hard way that the final 20 percent of a project is generally the most difficult. On our shelves at home, we might find more books read halfway than completely. The landscaping is never quite finished. At work, a salesperson doesn't get paid a commission for how many calls are made—the reward is for the sales that are closed. Procrastinators have trouble even starting things! Yet when we don't close well, we carry baggage that doesn't need to be ours. This baggage collects and weighs us down emotionally, and eventually physically.

I spent more than 20 years in the software development arena prior to founding the Institute for Leadership Excellence and Development. In the early years we had unmistakable cycles of pedal-to-the-metal, pizza-at-2:00 A.M. workdays near the end of a software release. This would be followed by a slower planning time, then a gearing up for another product's sprint to the finish. This cycle gave us time to recover from the toll of the release process.

In the mid-1990s, however, speed became the priority—"He who delivers first, wins!" This turned into shorter cycles and more frequent releases, which ultimately became a non-stop sprint. The result: each successive cycle carried more baggage such as software bugs, employee burnout, and overwhelmed customers who were given more than they could assimilate. In short, our software, our staff, and our customers were teetering on the edge of the fall-behind point.

What we had failed to realize is that to achieve long-term success, we needed to remember that each release is just one leg of an overall journey. Without that perspective, the fall-behind point was just a matter of time.

IT'S A VOYAGE

Life is a voyage. Any change is just one leg of the journey, albeit with both an ending and a beginning. Yet if you combine enough changes without giving yourself time to get the necessary perspective, the fall-behind point is a condition you will inevitably face.

How can you steer clear of the fall-behind point? Part of the answer lies in how you navigate the ending and the beginning, making sure you don't carry any more of that extra baggage than necessary. I call that process "closing well", and that's the subject of our next chapter.

CHAPTER FOUR

Closing Well

▼

IF YOUR COMPANY IS REORGANIZED and you end up with a different boss, there is an ending (your previous relationship with the old boss, your comfort level with his/her expectations, your informal agreements) and a beginning (new expectations, the potential need to re-establish credibility). If a downsizing action puts you on the streets, there is an ending (your job, any ego you had wrapped up in the position, security from a regular paycheck) and a beginning (new opportunities, the chance to re-assess what you want to do). If someone close to you dies, there is an ending (the person's life, his or her influence and companionship) and a beginning (the challenges of living without the person). For just about

Ultimately I had to choose: Am I going to dream my dreams or try to live them?

any change that blows your way, you can identify endings *and* beginnings associated with it. What I want you to consider at this point of our journey is the *ending* part of this equation. Your ability to avoid the fall-behind point depends heavily on how effectively this is done.

We typically think of mourning as appropriate for the major losses of our lives. There is value in considering the mourning process for lesser transitions as well. For example, after years of dreaming about starting my own company to help organizations solve problems through leadership development, I finally made the decision to leave my full-time job at ACNielsen. I had been toying with the dream for years as a part-time speaker, writer, and coach, but ultimately I felt I had to choose: Am I going to dream my dreams or try to live them?

Certainly, career decisions are big, but changes in employment are not generally situations most of us would consider grieving over, particularly if you think you are heading into a better situation. But as I prepared to leave ACNielsen, I actively applied this principle of closing well and mourning change. Before I even resigned, I blocked out time to specifically reflect on how much I would miss particular employees and customers, how much I would miss working on products I had put so much energy into over the years, and recalling the lessons I had learned during my time with the company.

When I gave my notice, I worked out an arrangement that allowed much more than the standard two weeks to help transition the new person in smoothly. I made a point to call or e-mail each of the people who came to mind that had helped me over the years, and in each communication I tried to relate what I appreciated about them or learned from them. The process took well over a month, but the net result was rewarding. I left with a sense of accomplishment—knowing that some pretty worthwhile things were accomplished during my nearly nine years there, and that some relationships were established that will last far longer than any product we developed. I closed well, and it felt great. However, there are plenty of situations in which I did not close well, and I still deal with those regrets.

One of my great high school memories was having the privilege of playing on a very successful basketball team. My senior year, the Morton Potters (yes, that was our name!) were 27-1 in a season that resembled the movie *Hoosiers*. The experience earned me a scholarship to play basketball at Northern Michigan University, an NCAA Division II school in the Upper Peninsula of Michigan. Tom Izzo, now the head coach at Michigan State University, was the assistant coach at Northern back then. I will never forget one of Tom's trademark impassioned speeches: "If you quit before the end of your four years, you will regret it for the rest of your life."

After three years of working hard, yet justifiably getting marginal playing time, I and my knees were feeling the toll. Realizing the Chicago Bulls would not be calling me, I started down the path toward "early retirement" even as Coach Izzo's words burned in the back of my mind. Rather than walking in and talking to the coaches, though, I just stopped showing up at informal team gatherings after the season ended my junior year. I mentioned to team members that I was not going to return, but I never sealed the closure with those who had invested so much in me. Late in the summer I received a letter from the head coach informing me that he understood I was not returning, so my scholarship was going to be given to someone else.

In the early months of my senior year, I began feeling the regret Coach Izzo had talked about. I was not only a quitter, but I quit in an irresponsible way. For years I deeply regretted the decision, and even now I use it as a personal motivator to always end well. In fact, a growing passion in my speaking, writing, and coaching is to help leaders structure their responsibilities and goals so they can someday end well.

Obviously, there are many changes in life which make my experiences seem trivial. Some changes occur so suddenly that they take months, maybe even years, to work through. But whether it's a relatively easy change, or a more complex one like losing your job or losing a spouse or being diagnosed with a life-threatening illness, the principle remains the same: Seek to close well in all of the changes that make up your life's journey. Seek to resolve each chapter before getting too far into the next.

Closing well takes time. There is no rush. In sailing, it is actually a big advantage to change directions (or *tack*) as quickly as possible. If the tack is performed too slowly, the boat catches too much wind and momentum is lost. For us humans, however, there is often little benefit to rushing. For the sake of perspective, let me suggest what I have seen work in the real world: Resolving the issues that accompany major life changes usually takes in the range of two years or more. If you are in the wake of one of these major changes, are you trying to sail through it too quickly? If you are close to someone on such a leg, could you be subtly trying to rush them?

You may find it helpful to do further study on this topic. J. Shep Jeffreys authored an easy-to-read book entitled *Coping with Workplace Change: Dealing with Loss and Grief*, which I recommend to you. Dr. Jeffreys worked with Elisabeth Kübler-Ross, who is perhaps best known for identifying the stages of loss and grief (denial, anger, bargaining, depression, and acceptance).

Different people resolve issues at different speeds. The message here needs to be clear: Take the time to truly work through the changes that blow your way, and don't rush the process. The more thoroughly you do it now, the more effective you'll be later on in the voyage.

CHAPTER FIVE

Choices and Expectations

The pessimist complains about the wind;
the optimist expects it to change;
the realist adjusts the sails.

WILLIAM ARTHUR WARD

EARLIER I PROPOSED *perspective* as the key word for managing change. Now I'm going to give you what I have found are two of the most powerful tools at our disposal for gaining the voyage mindset: *choices* and *expectations*.

On a moment-by-moment basis, we are making choices that shape our very existence. Many choices are so subtle or ingrained that we don't even consciously contemplate them. When choices turn into actions repeated over time, they become habits.

I recall when my oldest child went downhill skiing for the first time at age 7. After hours of classes and practice, he exclaimed, "Daddy, it's kind of weird. When I turn, my skis almost know what to do without me thinking about it! They just do the right thing!" You can view habits as choices we just don't spend much time thinking about! Constructive, consistent patterns regarding how we think about others, how we think about ourselves, and how we think about the future are powerful tools to help us weather changes.

Though some choices are made out of habit, others are so consequential that we labor over them, spending anxious days and sleepless nights wondering which option is *right*. There are no simple formulas to turn these difficult possibilities into easy decisions. However, regardless of the scope of our options, it is important to accept that deep within ourselves we indeed have the opportunity and the responsibility to take the helm, to make the necessary choices to deal with change.

SO, YOUR POINT IS?

Now I realize you might be thinking, *Well, duh! Everyone knows we have the power to choose! What's the big deal?* The big deal is that most of us know in our head that we have the ability to choose, but internally we often do not take responsibility for the choices we make. To illustrate, consider how we talk: "I wish I could do that." "I'm sorry, but I can't make it." "I could never speak in public." "She made me so upset." "I was just born that way, I guess."

Read those statements again. Is it obvious to you where the lie is in each of them? Do you see where such statements throw responsibility off of the person saying them and onto someone or something else? It may not be obvious to you if you haven't wrestled much with this principle of choice.

THE BITTER PILL

A wise person once told me to raise a red flag anytime I heard myself say, "I can't," "I have to," or "I wish," as these are words that often indicate I am avoiding responsibility and not reflecting the choices involved. It is a true statement that "I can't be as good of a basketball player as Kobe Bryant," but it is equally true that I could have made choices in my life to be a much better player than I am. It is true that "I have to die someday," but there are choices I can make that can affect the quality of my life. Is it more proper to say, "I can't make it to that meeting," or "I am not going to that meeting because I choose to (fill in the blank)"?

I invite you to take action and raise a mental red flag when you hear yourself saying, "I can't," "I have to," or "I wish." When it comes to truly assuming a voyage mindset, we must swallow the bitter pill of taking responsibility with our choices. Though it is tough medicine, it is the sailing equivalent of a motion sickness pill!

For more information on how our words and questions affect our attitudes, I strongly recommend *QBQ* by John G. Miller, available at www.qbq.com.

EXPECTING CHANGE

Expectations really turn out to be choices. We choose what our expectations will be regarding various areas of our lives. There are countless factors that drive our natural expectations of life, but when it comes right down to it, our expectations are within our control and we can choose to set them wherever we desire.

My experience is that most people do not expect change. Though William Arthur Ward attributes this to a pessimistic viewpoint (see the beginning of this chapter), I think a good number of optimistic people live this way.

We must not go through life with the expectation that things will stay the same.

We know intellectually that rapid change is a reality, but deep down we are often taken completely by surprise when change blows across our bow. It's someone else who is supposed to get laid off. Someone else is supposed to get that diagnosis. Bad things aren't supposed to happen to good people. How could this come up when everything was going so smoothly? How could the clients change their minds after we've gotten this far with the project?

The issue isn't that we have to be happy or excited about changes that blow our way. Blind optimism does not make a great sailor. Our call is to be Ward's realists—ones who sail with the expectation that things are going to change, and who assume the responsibility to turn into the wind, make the necessary adjustments (however radical they may be), and continue to live our lives when changes do occur. We don't know what the changes will be; we don't even have to like them when they show. But we must not go through life with the expectation that things will stay the same. And we must not play the victim when the changes appear.

CHAPTER SIX

Open to Opportunity

▼

CAN YOU THINK of someone in your workplace who always seems cool under stress? Suzanne Kobasa and Salvatore Maddi, authors of *The Hardy Executive: Health Under Stress*, studied leaders in stressful jobs who remained strong and healthy. One major trait shared by all the executives was the perception that change was an unavoidable challenge to master, rather than a threat. This has some parallels to the word picture in the Chinese ideogram for crisis, which combines both *danger* and *opportunity*. Doesn't that really capture the essence of change? Setting our expectations that change is a challenge to master—an opportunity for making things better—makes a big difference in how we navigate through it when it does arise.

Setting our expectations that change is a challenge to master makes a big difference in how we navigate through it.

Are you dealing with a job loss? You probably feel the danger, but how about the opportunity? While coaching people in job transition, I can see a vast difference in even the physical demeanor of people who face the challenge with an attitude of opportunity.

If this is an unnatural inclination for you, that is OK! It will likely feel like blind optimism at first as you force yourself to find a shred of opportunity in what appears to be a dark and dangerous storm. With persistence and practice, though, you can make progress towards having a positive predisposition toward change, recognizing that it can lead to opportunity. As we learn that changes can often be used to our benefit, we begin to realize this is not blind optimism at all!

ADDRESSING ATTITUDE

With realistic expectations in place, we are in a better position to maintain one of the key factors of managing change: our attitude. The link between attitude and performance is clear. Yet too often we find ourselves around people with less-than-inspiring outlooks when it comes to change. Skepticism, fear, distrust, and ambivalence can spread like a virus, infecting everyone exposed. Learning how to inoculate yourself from the influence of these attitudes is critical.

Without a doubt, attitude is a choice, and, indeed, it is a key factor in your ability to handle change. Do you realize it is one of the few things you actually have nearly complete control over? Chuck Swindoll has summed up the essentials we need to absorb into the depths of our being if we truly want to manage change well. Check this out:

> *The longer I live, the more I realize the impact of attitude on my life. Attitude, to me, is more important than facts. It is more important than the past, than education, than money, than circumstances, than failures, than successes, than what other people think or say or do. It is more important than appearance, giftedness, or skill. It will make or break a company . . . a church . . . a home. The remarkable thing is we have a choice every day regarding the attitude we will embrace for that day. We cannot change our past . . . we cannot change the fact that people will act in a certain way. We cannot change the inevitable. The only thing we can do is play on the one string we have, and that is our attitude. . . . I am convinced that life is 10% what happens to me and 90% how I react to it. And so it is with you . . . we are in charge of our attitudes.*[3]

First Lady Martha Washington similarly said, "I've learned from experience that the greater part of our happiness or misery depends on our dispositions and not on our circumstances."

Consider a change you are facing right now. According to both Swindoll and Washington, only a small percentage of what you're dealing with is the change itself; the rest is how you are reacting to it. So, how are you reacting to it? Do you see ways that you could think differently about the situation and recognize some opportunity?

As we discuss the issues of attitude and choices, we need to acknowledge that making choices inherently involves taking risks. Certainly many factors contribute to our willingness to take risks, including potential benefits, probabilities of success, and the costs of failure. Some people believe we make our choices based on which is greater: the perceived pleasure (benefits) or the perceived pain (risks).

We often avoid decisions by not objectively evaluating the hazards. Some of us run from the *costs of failure* without realizing how high the *probabilities of success* really are. Often the costs of failure are quite overstated! You might be a *ready risk taker*—a person who naturally accepts risks. By nature, I'm not one of those people—I have to force myself to risk, to honestly assess the factors and take a step forward even when a part of me inside screams "No!" Can you relate to that?

Your willingness to risk may involve understanding that there is something more important than just this change.

Let me be clear: This is not a call to make plans to bungee jump off a bridge tomorrow because you need to be more bold! However, I am encouraging you to take a look inside yourself to evaluate how honest you are with your choices. Ambrose Redmoon said, "Courage is not the absence of fear, but rather the judgment that something else is more important than fear." Perhaps your success at improving your reaction and willingness to risk involves understanding that there is something more important than just this change-event itself. What's more important is how it can be used to your benefit.

Refer back to the "Top Changes" you identified earlier in the book. With those in mind, ask yourself the following questions:

- Do I buy-into the "10 percent is what happens, and 90 percent is how I react to it" perspective?

- Are my responses filled with *can'ts, have-to's,* or *I wish's?*

- Do I tend to play it too safe when it comes to analyzing risks?

- Am I willing to start taking on a little more risk by stretching my comfort zone?

- Am I willing to work at more readily accepting what life throws me and setting my expectations accordingly?

Novelist J. H. Brennan said, "Almost everybody walks around with a vast burden of imaginary limitations inside his head." How you think about change can significantly influence how effectively you navigate through it. Take responsibility for your attitude about the specific transition, keeping your eyes open for opportunities that may be introduced. Soon the burden of the self-imposed limitations will be cast aside as you navigate your way through the change.

CHAPTER SEVEN

Confronting Control

▼

IT HAS BEEN SAID, "We don't mind change; we just don't like being changed!" There is some truth to that. "Being changed" implies that the change process is moving forward regardless of our approval. This brings up the critical issue of control.

I know of a commercial pilot who was as calm and cool in the cockpit as one could expect. But when this pilot was a passenger back in the cattle car class with the rest of us, he was a nervous wreck.

Then there are the leaders who are quite adept at sending out press releases and memos, but are terribly uncomfortable when publicly put on the spot with difficult questions. Rather than face real-time inquiries, they pick carefully selected questions from the magic fishbowl on the stage so they can respond with carefully scripted answers.

A common thread in both of these illustrations is control. When we are confronted with a change where we have limited control, we are faced with "being changed," and that can be a very uncomfortable position.

You have probably been encouraged at times to "let go" of a situation. *Letting go* is a nice little change-doctrine soundbite that we know is important, but that is so hard to practice in the real world. It's not just that we find it difficult to let go; indeed, most of us hate to let go. However, our problem is often that we don't even realize we're hanging on! How many times have you banged your head against a wall on a problem or issue that you just didn't have any control over? We fill our lives with worries, concerns, and ulcers that are not ours to have, yet we stubbornly hold onto them anyway.

Most discussions on the topic of control try to convince us to "let go" more often. Resisting changes we cannot control is definitely a key issue for most of us. However, I can't let this section go by without bringing up the other side of the argument. Consider this statement:

Anyone can learn to respond to change in a productive way.

Your reaction to change is totally within your control. Anyone can learn to respond to change in a productive, healthy way. Do you believe that? Do you honestly believe that *your* reaction to each of your "Top Changes" is totally within your control?

I do. I hope you eventually will as well. This principle is absolutely critical for us to effectively harness the winds of change. It is self-evident that we cannot control the changes that blow into our lives, but we can control our responses. The truth of this does not make the practice of it easy. I've been a believer of this principle for nearly a decade, and yet I still struggle to live it out.

So let's talk about how you can start practicing this principle in the real world. Consider the "Top Changes" you identified earlier in the book. As you look at each one, ask yourself these questions:

- *What aspects of this change do I definitely have control over?*

- *What aspects might I have some control over?*

- *What aspects do I definitely have no control over?* Be careful with this one for two reasons. First, we almost always have more control than we think. Make sure you see it clearly. Second, if we assume we do have control when we don't, we are needlessly worrying about something that cannot be changed.

- *What is the worst-case scenario for me if the uncontrollable parts of this change go bad?*

- *Am I willing to accept this worst-case scenario, if necessary?*

All of these questions have built-in challenges. The fact is, it's difficult to be objective about your own problems! You might try doing these exercises with the mindset that a close friend will be reviewing the results. For some of your transitions, you might even want to include a trusted friend or a mentor as a sounding board for this exercise. There is great benefit to objectively working through each of the questions for situations you are encountering right now.

The worst-case scenario question above is an important one. The exercise is most powerful when you can answer *Yes* to it. Getting to that point might require hours, even days or weeks. However, your mental and emotional buy-in to accepting a change even if it goes completely south is absolutely fundamental as part of your voyage mindset. Dale Carnegie's book *How to Stop Worrying and Start Living* says it this way: "Be willing to have it so." The quote is attributed to William James, the father of applied psychology. According to Carnegie, James felt it was important to be "willing to have it so because acceptance of what has happened is the first step in overcoming the consequences of any misfortune."[4] This does not mean you like the idea, are excited to see it happen, or promise not to weep and wail if it happens. It does, however, mean that you have weighed the possibility in the balance, and that, if the number is called, you know you aren't going to fall to pieces.

For those items that you have all or partial control over, it's time to put a plan together. I'm not talking about one of those lists that you scrawl on a scrap of paper and then lose by the next day. For big issues, I'm not opposed to pulling out a computer-based scheduling program or project management tool and treating it

> *For those items that you have all or partial control over, it's time to put a plan together.*

like a real project. For most issues, though, I make sure there is time blocked out on my calendar or an entry is put in an electronic to-do list that is in my face on a daily basis. Regardless of how you choose to keep track of your action plan, the following must be done:

1. Identify a specific "next step" within your control that you are going to take to address this challenge.

2. For each step, think through any "dependencies"—those things you are depending on occurring before you can finish your part—and then prioritize the tasks.

3. Assign a date that you will have this step completed by.

4. Make sure your action item list is always accessible. Make the choice to be reminded of (and annoyed by, if necessary) your commitments daily.

So far this is just basic action-item mantra. Here's where I diverge—right where most of us fail:

Block out time in your schedule to work on this!

So many times I have seen action items roll over from one day to the next. Be jealous with your work schedule. Plan time to do these important steps now, before your calendar gets filled with other commitments. Your schedule is one thing over which you must exercise a lot of control. If something creeps into your blocked-out time, reschedule it. In a sense, you could think of the voyage mindset as making you the project manager for your life!

Your schedule is one thing over which you must exercise control.

Before we leave this topic of control, I want to mention another tool I have used with great success to gain some ground in situations where it seems I am out of control. The tool is called a *Worry List*. The *Worry List* is definitely not a tool designed for everyday use. I compile a Worry List whenever I start to sense that overwhelmed feeling most of us know all too well. Though I might only do this exercise a couple of times a year, I have found there is something powerful in writing down your worries.

Here's what I do to create a *Worry List*. I open a word-processor and type something to the effect of:

TODAY'S DATE: _____

The following is a list of everything that I can possibly think of that I am worried about right now. I list these here because I am feeling overwhelmed and need to get some perspective.

There's nothing magical about that opening, but I think there are two benefits: it reminds you why you are going through this exercise (to get perspective), and it admits your feeling of being overwhelmed (an acknowledgment which, in itself, releases some pressure).

From there, I just start my fingers flying with worries that are on my mind. I like to use the outlining feature of Microsoft Word or the mindmapping capability of a product like MindManager from Mindjet. There is no right or wrong way to do a *Worry List*—you just need to learn what works for you. There's something therapeutic about going through the exercise. Identifying "next actions" for those items you think are most likely to be an issue is valuable, but you certainly don't need to do that for every concern.

Once you build a *Worry List* or two, you'll find it interesting to refer back to it someday. That's why I always make sure there's a date on the list. As you might expect, most of the worries turn out to be less than threatening, and some of them I can hardly even remember. That's perspective-building for your voyage mindset as well!

Lifelong Learning

▼

YOU WILL RECALL that this entire section is challenging you to take on a *voyage mindset*. We have talked about such key issues as perspective, choices and expectations, opportunity, attitude, and control. The final angle on the mindset change I am calling for is *lifelong learning*.

Following the sailing theme, I have a question. Do you think Dennis Conner was born a great sailor, or did he become one over the years? Despite the fact that Conner is the only skipper in the history of the America's Cup to lose the Cup twice, he is also the only one to have won it four times. Conner's chairman for the 1980 and 1983 campaigns, G. F. Jewett, Jr., said it well in a letter to *Sports Illustrated*: "In any sport top athletes like Dennis are there because of their dedication, integrity, and hard work." I noticed he didn't say "raw genius" or "unsurpassed brilliance."

I believe Dennis Conner to be a gifted person who, through much effort and devotion, became one of America's finest sailors. When you consider the technological changes that occur each year at that level of sailing, staying on top requires a commitment to continual learning—a relentless striving to improve.

When it comes to sailing the winds of change, I believe that some of us are more "change hardy" than others for a number of reasons.

Though genetics may have a fair amount to do with the difference, I personally believe that the experiences we have encountered (and learned from) during our journey through life are even more critical. For example, have you ever noticed that, generally speaking, people who have moved a lot tend to integrate into new settings quicker than the person who has just left home for the first time? Though the repeated moving most likely presented many challenges for those people, there were lessons learned during the process that net out to be a benefit.

So, good for those who have learned and bad for the rest of us? Not necessarily. As you can tell from the term, *lifelong learning* is all about a mindset that realizes that education does not stop when you receive your last diploma. In fact, it's much broader than just going to some seminars or workshops, or reading a book. It's a mindset that activates the learning process on a daily basis in everything we do. According to one expert, a redefinition of what it means to be "educated" is inevitable: "Increasingly an educated person will be somebody who has learned how to learn, and who continues learning."

Success in a world of change depends less on what you know, and more on what you can learn.

It's no longer as simple as how many letters you have after your name. Success in a world of change depends less on what you know, and more on what you can learn. Things will continue to change too quickly for anyone to be a guru in a specific area without a proactive program of continual learning. That's why I refer to this as lifelong learning.

It used to be that lifelong learners were your friends who refused to leave college—they just kept adding on new degrees! Now you are being summoned to be one yourself. Though you won't be sitting in university classrooms five days a week, you will have the mindset of a student—taking notes, experimenting with ideas in "the lab," talking to counselors about career planning, spending concerted time reading and writing while increasing your proficiency in some specific areas of study.

My guess is you're thinking something like, *OK, sounds great! I have this problem, though. I have a job, a family, a house, you know—responsibilities that students don't normally have. How do I find time for all this lifelong learning stuff?* It's a valid question. Let's face it—there are so many demands on our time these days that adding even another hour of commitment a week is asking a lot. Well, here are my answers to your insightful question:

First, I'll again mention blocking out time in your schedule. If you are not dedicating at least one hour a week of *Horizon Time*© (see the information about *Horizon Time* on page 74), you are cheating yourself and your company. You cannot afford to waste your weeks simply treading water from day to day without surfacing long enough to keep breathing. You must take control of your schedule. If you don't assume control of it, others will—and they'll be much less concerned about your growth than you are.

Second, find ways to use otherwise wasted time. For example, if you have a commute each weekday, are you using that time to learn? Audio books are a great way to make better use of your time. If cost is an issue, check out your local library, which often has a great supply of audio books on a range of topics. In addition, consider bringing material with you when going places that often have delays. For example, when I get a haircut, I usually bring some articles that I've torn out of a newspaper or magazine that I subscribe to. Rather than browsing an out-of-date *People*, I feed my mind with the learning I desperately need.

Third, make learning a part of your normal way of doing business. For example, when a project is completed (or a major phase of a project), conduct post-project reviews that emphasize what knowledge was gained, what you would do again, and what you would do differently next time. Here's another idea that I have been incorporating for years now: When someone resigns, I ask them to put together a few-page summary of what they learned during their time with our company. The process has many benefits, including helping the employee to "close well." However, I find that I also benefit when I read about their lessons. This parting ritual helps both parties become better informed.

Fourth, look for opportunities to learn new things. When you are reading a newspaper or a book, watching television, surfing the Internet, talking to other people, etc., do so with the mindset that you are there to find out something you didn't know before.

The fact is, we are all exposed to mountains of new knowledge on a weekly basis. The problem is, we don't benefit from the information because we often don't even realize we gained anything! We need to acknowledge what we have learned and file it in such a way that it can be applied at a later time. Passing it on to someone else is a great way to make it a part of your experience as well.

This lifelong learner mindset turns out to be really fun once you get started with it. I challenge you to view the world through the eyes of a student or an ever-curious child. You'll be amazed at the horizons that open up in front of you!

With this voyage mindset nicely in place, we are ready to move on to the next principle in managing personal change.

CHAPTER NINE

A Destination
and a Reason

▼

I HAVE THIS BUILT-IN "Dilbert-like" mechanism that shrieks a warning whenever I hear someone utter the term "mission statement." I don't believe I was born with this cynical sensor. Rather, I think my years of business experience have taught me that *mission statements* and *lip service* are all too often synonymous. However, my skepticism toward mission statements has waned some in recent years. Through the insight of mentors and authors, and my own personal experience, I have found that mission statements play a key role in our ability to handle change.

IF YOU DON'T KNOW WHERE YOU'RE GOING . . .

As we previously discussed, the underlying key for managing change is *perspective*. To accurately *"view things in their true relations or relative importance"* implies the ability to discern *relationship* and *importance*.

You are probably familiar with the old maxim: "If you don't know where you are going, any path will do." If you have nothing that can be held up as a standard of importance, you cannot hope to have perspective. Can you imagine sailing across a huge body of water without magnetic North as your reference, without measuring your progress against the stars, or without navigational instruments? Can you imagine trying to weave a sailboat through a dangerous reef without the benefit of detailed maps that clearly show the way through?

Let's get even closer to home. It's almost a cliché to say that there are not enough hours in a day to do what our lives seem to demand. When a well-intentioned request for your time is standing before you, what is the basis for your answer? If you are like most people, you make the decision according to whether or not you can fit the commitment in, or according to how you feel, rather than basing it on boundaries you have already set down regarding what is most important.

"IT'S WITHIN US"

All of us hold onto values, principles, and beliefs that are important to us. We all have at least some idea of what we want to do with our lives, though the picture is more clear for some than for others. In a sense, we all have mission statements within us that just need to be drawn out. In Stephen Covey's book *First Things First*, this concept is validated: "We don't invent our mission; we detect it. It's within us waiting to be realized."

FOCUS ON CHANGE MANAGEMENT

Let's look at how mission statements can help us navigate change. For the sake of example, let's say "Harry's" mission regarding work contained the following excerpt:

My goals are to achieve a position of respect and knowledge, to utilize that position to create useful technology solutions, and to play an active role in an organization committed to software development excellence.

Let's suppose Harry gets laid off. Is this the end of the world? Did he exit the only company that fit the filter of his mission statement? Hardly. Not only does a mission statement help provide perspective for a life change, but it can guide us toward a meaningful response. In the example above, the mission statement outlines the characteristics of companies that should be the focus of Harry's job search campaign: organizations committed to software development excellence.

When the winds of change are shifting and relentless, keeping your eyes on your personal mission statement provides a sense of balance—it helps define where you are headed and why you are going there. By reviewing our statements often, we can instantly recognize where we are off course and make small, lesser corrections that are not so turbulent.

In discussions with friends, colleagues, and clients, I have found that very few people have taken the time to develop their own personal mission statement. The process requires dedicated time for reflection and soul-searching. It forces us to ask questions we rarely consider: *Why am I here? What legacy do I want to leave? What is really important to me?* Answers to these questions are critical for staying on course in life, both in times of easy sailing and in vicious storms. If you have not drafted a mission statement, or if it has been a while since you dusted yours off, I strongly encourage you to treat this as a priority.

SO, WHERE DO I START?

Start the process by blocking out room in your schedule and getting away to a place where you can have some serious *think time* without interruptions. This doesn't have to be on a beach in the South Pacific! The key is that you are away from phones, e-mail, visitors, and any other things that would tempt your focus back on the urgency of today. This can be as easy as hiding in a conference room with a closed door or spending some quiet time at a library. With the current pace of life, I realize that even blocking out a half day for this could be a stretch for you. However, getting away from the day-to-day grind is very beneficial to this reflecting process.

Next, take some time to identify the primary roles you have in life. Your roles might include being a husband or wife, a father or mother, your position at work, your areas of responsibility in your community, etc. List each one that makes sense for your situation.

For each role, start asking the big-picture questions like:

• *What are the major contributions I want to make in this role?*

- *At the end of my life, what would I want people to say about how I fulfilled that role?*
- *What strengths do I have that make me particularly suited for this role?*

Beyond the roles, ask yourself other big-picture questions like:

- *What feelings do I want to have in my life? Peace? Confidence? Happiness? Meaning?*
- *If time, money, and resources were unlimited, what would I do?*
- *What do I really believe in terms of God, my relationship with Him, and concepts such as life after death?*

Your answers to these questions (and other questions you develop on your own) will begin to tell the story about your mission. If you would like more structure to help you create your personal mission statement, I recommend you use the "Mission Statement Workshop Appendix" in Covey's *First Things First*.[5] This is an excellent tool to jump-start your process.

DETECTING DRIFT

Regardless of how you go about developing your personal mission statement, make a commitment to review it on a regular basis. Some people return to it as often as weekly, but if you even look it over twice a year, there is benefit! This process doesn't have to take a lot of time. The key is to review your mission statement to help get your focus off the wind and the waves and onto the "horizon"—the long-term perspective that helps clarify if you are still on course.

You will find in your review sessions that slight updates to your mission statement are in order as your journey progresses. Don't consider your statement to be something that must be done perfectly the first time, then kept static forever. The more you use the tool and the longer you live, the more you will refine it to reflect desired course corrections.

You certainly do not need fancy software or tools to manage this process, but if you are technically inclined, there are many options available. The key is to use what works for you and actually do it!

LIFE IS A TERRIBLE THING TO WASTE

A sailing journey without a destination and a reason can be confusing and scary at best, and completely wasted at worst. Our lives are too short to sail in circles or drift meaninglessly. A personal mission statement can be an effective instrument to help you stay on course on your life journey.

CHAPTER TEN

An Accurate Set of Maps

▼

WHEN WE ARE IN UNFAMILIAR TERRITORY and need to go from "Point A" to "Point B", we could ask someone for directions, but that can get messy when people's memories are not quite to scale, so to speak. So we often consult a map.

A map is a beautiful thing because, for one, it is specific. I have always thought nautical maps are particularly interesting. There is so much information packed into the charts—depth and bottom type (e.g., 30 feet, muddy bottom), the color and number of buoys, the location of wrecked ships and other obstructions, references to landmarks like smokestacks and water towers. Similar to highway maps, there are various scales and degrees of detail. Mapping and tracking technology has been more widely used on boats than in cars thus far, allowing captains to have reliable and timely updates on current location, course, and distance to fixed points.

It is generally understood that maps are accurate as well. When they aren't, it usually is because they are simply outdated. However, even though we accept maps as accurate, no one truly mistakes them for reality. They are simply two-dimensional representations of reality.

MINDSET MAPS

Just as there are maps we use to navigate on land and on sea, there are mindset maps we use to navigate how we view the world beyond simply the physical terrain. These are often referred to as paradigms, mental models, and configurations. I prefer the term *mindset map* because it helps build a bridge between our understanding of maps in the real world and maps in the context of how our minds work. Regardless of whether or not you completely accept all the theory about mindset maps, they can be a helpful model for explaining why people react to change in different ways.

In short, here's the theory: We all have created mindset maps which represent our understanding and interpretation of the world around us. Our typical decision-making process can be thought of as simply data from the outside world being filtered and analyzed by the applicable mindset map(s). We use a countless number of maps on a daily basis, covering everything from how to deal with a certain team member when they are upset, to how to drive our cars when two lanes merge into one, to our personal biases of certain people based on race, gender, age, etc. Though there are many maps, there is usually a dominating map often referred to as the *personal map* that carries the general theme of our lives. Based on how we have drafted our mindset maps over the years, our decisions end up being quite consistent and even predictable once a map is correctly read.

UNMET NEEDS

The theory continues by suggesting that maps are generally fueled by one or more unmet needs that we are trying somewhat desperately to make up for. Different experts use different descriptions of needs, but here is a list for our consideration:

*We want to **Live** (physical needs which, if denied, would cause death).*
*We want to **Love** and **Be Loved**.*
*We want a sense of **Belonging** to someone and something.*
*We want a **Purpose** in our lives, a reason for being.*
*We want to **Become** more, to grow and progress.*
*We want to **Feel Important**, to be respected for who we are and what we do.*

We want **Variety,** *to experience many different things so that we may actually experience life.*
We want to be **Competent** *in the things we do.*
We want to be **Safe** *within our physical and social environment.*[6]

If you combined these needs into a pie chart and reflected a person's proportionate neediness to each, you would have what is often referred to as a "Need Wheel."

Imagine a man whose primary need is to be *Competent* and *Feel Important.* You can guess what he is like to work with. His maps would be tailored to make sure all incoming information is filtered accordingly, and his decisions would reflect whatever is necessary for him to be perceived as competent and feel important.

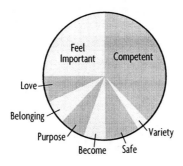

How about the woman whose driving need is *Variety*? When she *does* show up for work (you know, when she isn't skydiving, scuba diving, traveling, etc.!), she is probably not the one you can depend on to finish a long-term project.

TYING IT BACK TO MANAGING PERSONAL CHANGE

Based on this short introduction to the topic, you might guess that the way you react to change is heavily determined by your mindset maps. How would "Mr. Competent and Important" respond to change? Sounds like a potentially threatening situation to me! Do you want to roll out change to "Miss Variety?" No problem! Bring it on!

On the serious side, consider America in a post-September 11 condition. Our collective *Safe* wedge has expanded to dominate the wheel. You want to talk about extending wire-tapping laws prior to the terrorist attacks? Forget about it. Now that we have suffered such terrible devastation, though, we will entertain a lot of ideas as long as they help meet our newly increased felt-need for safety.

If the terrain changes but you refuse to modify your mindset maps accordingly, the gap between reality and the maps gets wider and wider. Granted, there are *always* gaps between the inner and outer realms. But the further your mindset map gets from the real world, the greater your odds are for a crisis. Eventually reality causes an *unresolvable bind* [7]—a situation where the pain of trying to solve problems with the outdated map becomes so overwhelming that you are forced to *modify the map*. Eventually reality wins.

THE LESSONS FOR US

I have found the concept of mindset maps to be very helpful on a number of fronts. First, it continually enables us to discover the blind spots we may have due to faulty biases, assumptions, or hidden agendas. When I am in situations where I sense anger, anxiety, or other strong emotions building up, I now have a tool that can help me analyze why I am feeling that way. What *need* is being threatened in the situation? Is it truly being threatened, or am I just not seeing things accurately? I'm finding my physical and emotional *warning lights* are opportunities to keep my maps up-to-date.

The most difficult behaviors to change are those responsible for past success.

Second, because understanding mindset maps helps you interpret the reactions of others, your ability to assist people in dealing with change can be greatly enhanced. If you get proficient at recognizing what is driving a person, you can begin to anticipate how they will react to change.

Third, there is an ironic truth that *the most difficult behaviors to change are those responsible for past success.* At first that doesn't seem to make sense. However, in the context of mindset maps, consider what happens through this example: A new manager finds his team is behind schedule as they near a deadline. He decides to enforce required overtime, including nights and weekends. Sure enough, the team delivers, and he notes the successful conclusion. When the next deadline nears, he calls the same play, working his team to exhaustion to hit the deadline. Same behavior, same results. However, eventually his team catches on to this. Some burn out and leave. Some just pace themselves until the inevitable push at the end. Eventually this behavior introduces negative results. If the manager fails to recognize this, he might very well completely destroy his team.

The lesson for us here is to constantly take an open-minded look at our assumptions when analyzing issues. Have a built-in bias that challenges assumptions—your own and those of others.

MOVING FORWARD

Here are my challenges for you, now that you have Mindset Mapping 101 under your belt:

- *Spend some time reflecting on what you think might be your driving needs (refer to the needs list above). What would the wedges of your Need Wheel look like?*

- *Spend some time reflecting on recent situations where you were very angry or anxious due to a change. Based on your needs analysis above, what were your maps telling you at the time? In retrospect, were you seeing things accurately?*

- *Review your list of major changes back on the first pages of this book. Are there mindset maps you need to modify to better reflect reality? Are you prepared to do so?*

Every sailor knows that a journey through difficult conditions and unknown territory is impossible without an accurate set of maps. I trust this material on mindset maps has challenged you to consider your maps and encouraged you to start the process of remapping where necessary. If you would like to read more on the subject of mindset maps, I highly recommend *The Change Navigator* by Kurt Hanks.

CHAPTER ELEVEN

A Trustworthy Crew

▼

I HAVE ALWAYS BEEN AMAZED by stories about people who sail around the world by themselves. It's not that I don't enjoy keeping my own company, but I just think time would grow long floating around strange places without someone to share the experience with, to back me up when I was exhausted or ill, or to lend a hand when conditions were bigger than I could handle alone. It could be that all of these challenges are the incentives for the solitary sailors! I just know the long solo journey is not for me.

Some people run their lives solo. Part of our American heritage is the pioneer—the person who risked life and livelihood to face new lands and conditions, often on his own or in small clusters with other pioneers. In our globalized business world that relies on partnerships and cooperation, it is becoming increasingly difficult to succeed while living a life that does not rely heavily on interdependent relationships.

In this climate of high change and uncertainty, I believe it is more important than ever to have a trustworthy crew—one or more people who are committed to you for the journey. These are people who support you regardless of the successes and failures you rack up. People who truthfully and lovingly confront you with concerns, and who openly celebrate victories with you. A trustworthy crew makes all the difference in sailing, and it is equally important in your personal life as well.

MORE THAN JUST FRIENDS

Regardless of whether we are socially awkward computer geeks (I say this with respect, as that is my heritage) or gregarious salespeople, we need to have at least a couple of people we can truly call friends. People who are more than social acquaintances. Who we relate to at a deeper level.

Consider the following questions:

Who are the first people that come to mind as being part of your trusted crew? Name them.

If you needed a sounding board for your thoughts/concerns regarding, let's say, an intensely personal issue, could you go to one or more of these people? Would they welcome such interaction?

Would you feel comfortable talking to one of more of these people about your fears? About the things that keep you up at night that no one else normally knows about? Once again, would they welcome such interaction?

If one or more of these people saw something in your life that concerned them, would they bring it to your attention in a constructive way, or just overlook it because they wouldn't want to judge or offend you?

If you can answer *Yes* to most of those questions about at least one other person, your ability to survive in a high-change environment is greatly increased. My contention is that most professionals don't have such people in their lives, however. We have neighbors, friends, work associates, and folks with whom we socialize. But for a myriad of reasons, a growing number of us are becoming increasingly isolated.

We need people in our life who will tell us when our breath is bad! We need someone who is willing to keep us accountable to agreed-upon goals if we ask them to; someone who sees through the smiles and knows we are struggling over something, perhaps even before discussing it. We need someone who will believe in us after everyone else has abandoned ship.

I have heard the *crew* concept talked about in terms of your own *personal board of directors*. I think that concept is sound, particularly if you consider it in terms of the more business-oriented aspects of your life such as financial and career decisions. Perhaps one of these people could serve on a more personal, emotional level as well.

WANT ADS FOR CREW MEMBERS?

If you can't honestly say you have the trustworthy crew I'm speaking of here, I don't have any quick fixes for you. Commitment of the type I am calling for is not something that is built up overnight or solved through the Personals section in the newspaper! However, if you are committed to establishing such a valuable support structure for your life, here are a couple of ideas for you:

Develop a list of people you think could fit into a crew member role as I have defined it.

_____

_____

_____

_____

After some consideration, select one or two of the people from the list and sit down with them one-on-one to talk about this concept. Share with them that you are interested in a deeper level of accountability and trust. Be specific with expectations—of yourself and of them. It could be that they are quite willing to help out but were waiting for "permission." It could also be that they aren't up for this level of commitment, which is fine. Better that they are honest about it upfront than that they disappoint you later.

When you are confronted by a crew member, take it seriously. A typical American mindset is that it's most polite for others to mind their own business, even after we give them permission to step in. You can go a long way in building the crew member relationship by honestly listening to feedback and acting on it when applicable.

The seas under us and the storms above us are changing too rapidly to sail completely solo anymore. The need for a trustworthy crew is more important than ever. Building these relationships takes time and commitment. I challenge you to set a goal for the next 12 months to enhance the quality and quantity of your crew. Your ability to manage change in the coming years may depend on it.

CHAPTER TWELVE

When the Weather Gets Rough

▼

THOUGH THE TEMPESTS we face are real, there are periods of calm between storms. It could be that you are in the middle of a big storm right now—and the reality of sunny, peaceful days is a distant memory. Or it could be you feel like the whole case is overstated since your life is rather calm right now. Regardless of how extreme the current weather conditions are, the principles discussed thus far have value in your journey. This section, however, is devoted specifically to those times in our lives when the winds and waves are especially fierce.

KNOW YOUR POSITION

A recent sailing outing in Door County, Wisconsin, was one to remember. My sailing buddies, Jim and John, were on board along with two friends for a weekend of solving the world's problems while sailing in the beautiful waters of Green Bay. We sail up in Door County most every summer and have learned to navigate by sight due to the proximity of land on all sides. On this particular Saturday morning we began our two-day sailing trip from Sturgeon Bay despite threatening skies and a forecast for rain. "Hey, what's a little rain?" we said.

We knew we should make it to Egg Harbor in less than five hours. After an hour of motoring through a channel, we entered the body of water named Green Bay. The cold winds were really starting to pick up, and our promised rain began to fall. We put our sails up, which immediately caught the gusting winds, leaning the boat over with a pretty good heel. In the next 30 minutes, we got caught in driving rain and the waves became more menacing. As it turns out, Green Bay is relatively shallow, so it doesn't take much for substantial wave action to build. We reduced our sail, which essentially leaves you with a smaller area exposed to the wind, making it easier to control the boat. However, we were still having trouble keeping the boat pointed to our desired course, so we decided to drop all sails and fire up the diesel.

While Jim was trying to steer our 34-foot Hunter sailboat, I was maneuvering around, making sure we kept good record of our progress. Between the rain and the fog, we were unable to navigate by sight. We might have been worried at that point except for three beautiful letters: GPS! The boat was equipped with a navigation unit which allowed us to electronically get accurate readings of our position. Every 15-30 minutes, I took a reading and marked it on a map. Our crew was beginning to wonder if we should turn around and head back to Sturgeon Bay as lightning had now started to dance in the rumbling clouds. The skies on the horizon appeared to be a little lighter and our destination seemed achievable, so we proceeded.

Through our tracking, I was able to verify we were making progress. When Jim began to feel ill, I took the helm and was surprised at how focused I had to be to keep on a direct course to Egg Harbor. There were no other boats in sight—a rarity for these waters. By the time we ended up at our destination some seven hours later, we all well understood what the phrase *chilled to the bone* means! We were cold, wet, and exhausted, yet felt a certain amount of victory at having braved the closest thing to our own *Perfect Storm*—and making it there alive!

KEEP A WATCH ON YOUR ENVIRONMENT

That sailing trip illustrates a number of lessons for when the change-storms of life hit you. The first lesson is the need to continually review your position, course, and conditions. The life equivalent of this is regularly asking some specific questions:

- *What is a one-sentence summary of how my life has been lately?*
- *Based on my mission statement and short-term goals, how am I proceeding?*
- *Are there any* course corrections *(decisions, attitude adjustments, actions I need to take, etc.) to get back on track?*
- *What have the* wind conditions *of my life been like lately? Am I getting close to the* fall-behind point?
- *Considering my schedule in the coming days and weeks, what is my best guess at the* change forecast? *Is high change likely in the near future?*

A good time to ask these questions is during your weekly review of your to-do's, appointments, and (if applicable) personal mission statement. These questions help build a bridge between the reality of today and your desires for the future. You might consider keeping a journal (electronic or on paper) to track your progress and issues over time. As with the Worry Lists talked about previously, being able to refer back to notes from past review sessions can be of great advantage.

By understanding how close you are to the fall-behind point, you benefit by early detection. Also, if you know some serious change is forecasted to be blowing your way in the near term (for example, you know a project is likely to be delayed, causing increased workload), you might choose to delay some personal change plans to avoid overloading yourself. For example, in mid-January one year I discovered I had put on about 10 pounds since the middle of the previous year. Because I had a number of rather major transitions going on at work and at home, I decided to not put personal emphasis on losing those pounds until I had made it through to the other side of the changes. I know myself well enough that I would just be pushed way too close to the edge of the fall-behind point if I started dieting during that time.

I challenge you to take the time to reflect on your current position, course, and conditions. This exercise, done regularly, can help keep you from reaching the fall-behind point and thus allow you to make minor course corrections earlier. Not a bad idea since it is true that the best time to change is before you have to!

STAY IN SAFE WATERS

Ironically, the safest place for a sailboat in rough weather is usually in the deepest waters. In my earlier sailing story, heading back to Sturgeon Bay would not have been a good idea considering the weather and conditions. The winds would have been *pushing* our boat, making it more difficult to control than when heading into the wind. Also, as we sailed closer to shore, the water would have been more shallow, so the odds of running aground were higher.

When high change hits your life, your first instinct might be to run: "Let me go back to how it used to be!" However, my counsel to you is to remember the sailing principle that the safest waters are the deepest. Fleeing change rarely works. Staying in the wind can sometimes be your ticket for finding opportunity through it.

TACK WHEN NECESSARY

One of the primary skills a sailor requires is knowing how to *tack* the boat. A tack is a change in direction that allows you to keep making progress without heading into the wind. Motor-boaters rarely have to worry about this issue—they just point their vessel, hit the gas, and head to their destination. Often tacking seems like a detour—a route you are almost compelled to take, but not generally the most direct one desired.

Life similarly throws variations into our plans. A phrase I saw on a coffee cup has stuck with me: *Learn to enjoy life's detours.* The detours in life can cause impatience, broken dreams, and frustration. But what if we could learn to appreciate them? What if we could find a way to be content no matter the route that personal change puts us on?

The next time the winds shift so that you need to tack to make progress, remember the line about life's detours. You might begin seeing detours as opportunities for change, which benefits you in the long run.

CHAPTER THIRTEEN

When the Weather
Remains Rough

▼

ON DECEMBER 14, 1994, American Eagle flight 3379 was descending toward the airport at Raleigh, N.C. At the controls was pilot Michael Patrick Hillis, who had joined American Eagle after previously being asked to leave Cincinnati-based ComAir for tensing up when things went wrong. As *U.S. News and World Report* relates: "At exactly 30 seconds after 6:33 P.M., two minutes and 4 miles from the airport, a panel light in the cockpit lit up. Hillis and his copilot, Matthew Sailor, had been trained to recognize the light as a signal that an engine had quit. Quickly, they set about determining which one. In doing so, however, they forgot about flying the plane." The plane crashed shortly afterwards. The conclusion from investigators: "Neither of the plane's engines had failed at all. Most likely, the light was faulty."[8]

There is a lesson we can all learn from this tragic accident. The *change* introduced in the cockpit of that commuter plane was not trivial—concern was warranted, and modifications to current plans were necessary. *But they forgot to keep flying the plane.*

That last sentence haunted me for a while after reading it. How could the pilots possibly have stopped paying attention to the job of keeping the plane airborne? After some reflection, I see now that it's not all that surprising. I talked to a student pilot on my staff at the time who echoed that this is a big point brought up during flight school because it *is* such a problem. Crisis has a way of consuming our attention.

STAY IN CONTROL OF THE BOAT

The lesson for us is that when a major change threatens to capsize your life, remember the simple phrase: *Keep sailing the boat*. Major changes can be traumatic, and they can hold you hostage every moment of your waking day. But you need to get out of bed in the morning, eat something, and go about life. It's the equivalent of putting one foot in front of the other when you seem too overwhelmed to do so. But you need to do it. Lives can be devastated when you forget to keep sailing the boat.

By the way, if this particular section is speaking to you, you are in good company. Every time I give this talk live, audience members approach me afterwards and say this is one of the ideas they most needed to hear. You might be surprised to learn how many people are struggling to get out of bed most mornings. If this isn't you, but you manage people, I ask that you consider that someone on your staff right now could be struggling with "sailing the boat." Perhaps that explains some of the problems you have noticed?

REDUCE HEELING BY TURNING INTO THE WIND

Even if you haven't been on a sailboat, you have probably seen pictures of boats leaning way over with one side seemingly about to dip into the water while the other edge flies high above. Sailors call this *heeling*. Sailboats are remarkably engineered to take advantage of heeling with a minimum possibility of capsizing. However, there are times when the best thing to do is to reduce the heel to sail more efficiently.

I was surprised when I learned that you reduce heeling by turning the boat *into* the wind as opposed to *away* from it. When it comes to dealing with change in our lives, I think the principle holds true as well. When changes make us tipsy and we are nearing the fall-behind point, the temptation is often to run for cover. As I mentioned in the section on tacking, running isn't always a bad idea, but it also isn't always the best idea. Turning into the wind—looking it in the eye, being *"willing to have it so"*—then making the necessary course corrections based on your destination and reason for sailing (your personal mission statement, goals, and objectives), is generally the trustworthy strategy in sailing and in life.

REDUCE YOUR SAIL

I mentioned in the Door County sailing story about reducing the sail when the winds were so strong. Reducing sail area helps a boat to not be overpowered by the wind, thus giving the helmsman more control over the vessel.

My equivalent lesson for us is learning to reduce our exposure when we are under heavy winds. Often this means learning to say "No" to the well-intentioned things which come our way. Do you feel comfortable saying "No" when the situation warrants it? Have you learned how to say "No" but still be helpful to the requester? Do you have objective criteria for when it is appropriate and reasonable to say "No"?

Many time-management curriculums include emphasis on the issues of *urgency* and *importance*. Have you ever thought about this? How much of your day is spent doing urgent things rather than things which are important? Obviously, many urgent things are also important, but not all of them. *Important* is defined as tasks which further your mission, goals, and objectives.

Rather than drill on the whole time-management aspect of managing change, here's my challenge for you: Take a time-management course this year. Whether it is in a classroom setting, or a book or tape series on the topic, invest in—and use—a good time-management curriculum. If you want a helpful book on the topic, check out David Allen's *Getting Things Done: The Art of Productivity*. In addition, the Institute for Leadership Excellence and Development (**www.i-leadonline.com**) offers a powerful and practical workshop and keynote presentation on the topic that has helped many people over the years. Consider contacting us to schedule one for your leadership team, department, or company.

In any case, take action on this challenge soon. Remember: Our ability to handle the peaks of change-storms can be greatly increased when we learn to minimize our exposure to things which are not essential.

FIX YOUR EYES ON THE HORIZON

If you have ever been on a rocking boat and you have any susceptibility to motion sickness, you may have learned the trick of keeping your eyes on the horizon. Something very confusing goes on in our bodies when the inner ear tells the brain that we're being tossed all around, but the eyes do not verify the movement. When we watch the horizon, the body seems better able to regain its equilibrium, which eases that queasy feeling in your stomach.

When you hit the fall-behind point from being rocked by relentless changes, remember to fix your eyes on the horizon (see information about Horizon Time on page 74). Get back to your personal mission statement and goals to remind yourself of what this whole trip is about. Remember that, as hard as this is, it's just one leg in the journey of your life. Getting your eyes off of the wind-swept waves and onto the horizon can make a substantial difference in how you handle life's most difficult storms.

RADIO FOR HELP

Whether your boat is in danger or someone needs CPR, a common principle for emergency situations is to call for help. For some reason, many of us have problems asking for help. Often the scope of the problem doesn't matter, we just won't seek assistance. There are people around you who are willing to help you through your difficult times in ways you might never expect. When you find yourself in the middle of the storm, or even when you see the storm approaching, open your mind to the possibility of calling out for help. Then do it.

CHAPTER FOURTEEN

Taking Care of the Captain and the Boat

▼

AN IMPORTANT FACTOR in your ability to effectively manage change for the long haul has to do with how well you take care of yourself. There's a principle of war that essentially says that the greatest victories are the battles that are never fought. They are the conflicts that are anticipated—and conquered—long before the tension rises to the point of battle.

If you have ever struggled with motion sickness, you know that when you start to feel ill, it's too late to take the medication—the time to take it is before you get on the boat. Likewise, it is difficult to start harnessing change productively once you are pounded by waves and chilled to the bone from the cold, driving rain. One of the greatest keys to successfully managing personal change lies in your preparation and the habits formed before the storms hit. Taking care of yourself so that you are ready to take on the tough times is what this section is all about.

FORCE REFLECTION

There was a day when life seemed to pass by at the pace of a horse and buggy. There was time to smell the roses along the way. As the pace at which we live is now more like a supersonic jet, the roses are just a blur! In order to assimilate all the events and changes of our lives and keep them in perspective, we must get off the jet and figure out how the pieces of our lives fit together.

This sort of perspective-building activity doesn't happen automatically for most of us. Some people tend to be more introspective than others. The less contemplative might find this whole topic almost nauseatingly irrelevant, seeing introspection as a waste of time. How each of us approaches the opportunity for reflection will greatly differ. The key is that you take time to reflect in a way that yields the necessary benefit.

Reflecting is a fundamental activity of true learning.

Reflecting is a fundamental activity of true learning. How can we learn if we don't take time to analyze what we learned, to consider how we might have done things differently, and to assess where we really are? How do we know if we are progressing, improving, growing?

SO, HOW DO I START?

Here's something I started doing many years ago that anyone can do—I call it *Horizon Time©*. Pick a time once a week during your normal working hours. The duration should be no less than an hour and probably doesn't need to be more than two. If you have an office, shut the door. If you work in a cubicle, hide in an empty office or conference room. If you absolutely, positively cannot take work time to do this, then block out the hours at home before work during the week, or before the family gets moving on the weekend. Block off the time and make it non-negotiable. If you absolutely must cancel it, reschedule it immediately. The message here is to make it happen.

Bring your laptop if you have one, or a pad of paper if you don't. Don't take or make calls, don't work on e-mail, and don't fall asleep! Use the time to scan the horizon, to gain perspective, to take a deep breath away from the day-to-day storms and meeting overload. During this time, I typically read from the stack of journals I have been meaning to get to. Occasionally I will pull up a document on my laptop that lists my dreams, goals, and personal mission statement. I'll read through each one and sometimes make a note about how I'm doing against those items since the last time I reviewed them.

How you use this time is up to you. Some people will just want to journal about what is going on. This is a great time to review your "current position, course, and conditions" or create a Worry List. The options are many. I have found the challenge is just setting aside the time and following through on making it happen.

TAKE CARE OF YOURSELF

Though "take care of yourself" sounds like a message from a mother, most of us still need to be told this today. I've broken this section out into four areas—taking care of ourselves physically, emotionally, intellectually, and spiritually. These categories represent essential areas of needs which must be fed and maintained for us to live balanced, effective lives. Lives that have the stamina and fortitude to keep moving toward the destination regardless of the changes around us.

It is important to note that each area is vitally important. As Stephen Covey says:

> Any one of these needs, unmet, reduces quality of life. If you're in debt or poor health, if you don't have adequate food, clothing, and shelter, if you feel alienated and alone, if you're mentally stagnant, if you don't have a sense of purpose and integrity, your quality of life suffers. Vibrant health, economic security, rich, satisfying relationships, ongoing personal and professional development, and a deep sense of purpose, contribution, and personal congruence create quality of life.[9]

PHYSICALLY

It is self-evident that we need to take care of ourselves physically in order to thrive throughout the journey. I'm not going to put you on guilt trips about eating right or exercising enough. You know yourself and what needs to be done in those areas, if anything. Nothing I write here will cause you to change. That must come from within you, and I am increasingly impressed with the number of people who are taking responsibility for their health by eating better and exercising regularly. Once you make the decision to truly start taking your physical health seriously, make sure to block out time in your schedule to accommodate your commitment.

I do want to spend an additional moment, though, challenging you to become more aware of your *Personal Instrument Panel©*. I alluded to this briefly during the discussion on mindset maps. How do you know if you are off course? You certainly do not want to wait until you hear the rocks scraping the hull of the boat! In life, you do not want to wait until you hit the rocks either.

In my life, I have learned to trust my wife Sara and her ability to read me like a book. She can look me in the eyes and discern if I am off track. I have learned to trust her intuition, regardless of whether or not I recognize a problem. In addition, I have learned that if I am short with the kids, then I am probably off course. My experience is that my three children under the age of eight often act like children under the age of eight! When I too easily get irritated at them acting their age, I need to re-evaluate.

Each of us has a sophisticated early-warning system that, if followed, will help us realize we are physically and/or emotionally near overload. Take the time to learn what your personal lights and alarms are, and to develop additional ones where necessary. Then take action when they go off.

EMOTIONALLY

The warning lights and alarms discussion carries over into the emotional realm as well. Beyond that, I would like to mention three additional items that can help you take better care of yourself emotionally:

Wipe Out Worry

Worry is the anchor of my sailing metaphor. Anchors are a great accessory on the boat when used correctly. However, if you drag an anchor behind you while you are trying to set sail, you can expect to be slowed down or even stopped. Worry is the dragging anchor of our beings. Studies abound on the physical toll worry takes on us. I would give you more details, but it might cause you to worry more!

The Worry List tool mentioned previously has proven to be a good instrument in my life. Worry is a concern that is not being acted upon. An anchor is excellent when used as intended, and worry can be useful as a warning sensor that a problem might be looming. If we sit and fret about the problem without taking real action, we end up wallowing in worry. If we face the problem and realize there's nothing we

Each of us has a sophisticated early-warning system that, if followed, will help us realize we are physically and/or emotionally near overload.

can do, then we take the action of letting it go. If you don't let it go, then you are frozen in the inactivity of anxiety.

The next time your worry sensors go off, consider for a moment what action you can take right now to address the worry. If there isn't anything you can do at the moment, then your worry is wasted, and it is stealing precious energy from you the longer it goes unchecked.

Watch That Thought

I am continually amazed at the garbage we allow to pile up in our minds in the form of negative thoughts. They easily become self-fulfilling prophecies. Studies have proven that upbeat, positive thinkers are more likely to succeed. There are techniques available to help us use the power of our minds to overcome negative thinking. Learn to better manage your thoughts, and you'll be helping the captain more effectively sail the boat!

Taking Yourself Seriously

Most of us tend to take ourselves way too seriously. Lighten up! I know so many excellent business leaders who are perfectionists to a fault. Allow yourself a mistake every once in a while. During this calendar year, learn to laugh at yourself more easily. There's no need to take ourselves so seriously, so I'll say it again—lighten up!

INTELLECTUALLY

As we discussed in the mindset map section, intellectual honesty is a key skill for managing change. This means being committed to keeping your mindset maps reflecting reality as much as possible. It means looking at situations and focusing on facts as they are, without the selective filtering that is natural for most people. Feeding your mind to keep it challenged and engaged should be a top priority.

SPIRITUALLY

We all have a need within us to possess some deep sense of purpose and contribution. The spiritual side of our being thrives on the fulfillment of this need. Throughout history there are countless examples of people who have managed some of the most extreme changes possible and thrived because of their faith in God. Take time to consider if you are giving this side of your life enough focus, remembering that true success is possible when all four dimensions of your life are equally nurtured. My personal experience is that this single factor has made the most radical difference in my ability to deal with life's changes. If that is not your story, maybe it is time to reconsider this.

By the way, not only can such a pursuit help provide answers for your "what's the meaning of life" questions, but there is increasing evidence that people who are committed to their religious faith reap other benefits such as lower blood pressure, more inner peace, better marriages, and better overall health.

CHAPTER FIFTEEN

Lifelong
Learning, Again!

▼

EARLIER I DISCUSSED how lifelong learning is an important part of the "voyage mindset." In order to take care of the captain and the boat, there are two particular areas of lifelong learning to consider: your career and knowledge management.

YOUR CAREER

Estimates vary as to how many different jobs we will most likely have during our careers, but there is complete consensus on this: the one-cycle career path of working for a single company until age 65 is gone for good. According to John Challenger, executive vice president at the Chicago-based outplacement firm Challenger, Gray, and Christmas, the average person will work five or six jobs before they retire. Regardless of how accurate the estimates are, the message is that you are going to be learning many different industries, and working with different product lines and technology bases. From strictly a career standpoint, the need to embrace a lifelong learning mindset is critical.

Many companies are putting greater emphasis on training their employees. Two ideas suggested by the *Wall Street Journal* are: use employer education benefits and start a career-development fund.[10] According to William M. Mercer, Inc., more than 90 percent of large and midsize employers provide financial assistance for job-related education, but surprisingly, only a small number of employees take advantage of this benefit. If you are not using this benefit at your job, you are walking away from money.

The idea of the career-development fund is to take the monetary part of training into your own hands. Some career consultants recommend saving 5-10 percent of your salary in a fund which is solely used to develop your career. This money can then be used to acquire new skills that employers might not be willing to pay for.

MANAGING KNOWLEDGE

There are a staggering number of instruments and services available to today's skippers to do everything from steering the boat and forecasting the weather to developing racing strategies. Information overload is a cliché for us as leaders today. One of our key challenges is how we will stay in touch, which tools and processes we'll use to acquire information, and how we'll retain the information for future reference. In the spirit of lifelong learning, this issue is key for us to be successful in a high-change environment.

Here are a few hints I can share from personal experience. Life seems way too busy for me to spend the amount of time reading that I feel is necessary to keep up. Because of this, I have been working on ways to maximize the reading time I do have. I have found services such as Executive Book Summaries to be an excellent resource for staying in touch with the latest issues, trends, and techniques in management literature. Each Executive Book Summary is a condensed summary of the top business books of our time, with two to three summaries delivered monthly. For books which seem especially relevant, I may choose to go out and buy the full book. But I usually get enough out of the summaries themselves to start applying some of the concepts. Executive Book Summaries are published by Soundview (for more information, check them out on the Web at **www.summary.com**).

My thirst for summaries does not end there. I am finding the online version of many newspapers and industry magazines a valuable tool as well. If you are interested in staying plugged in to companies dealing with change effectively, check out the online version of Fast Company magazine at **www.fastcompany.com**. If you have a palm-sized device, you can use a service such as AvantGo (**www.avantgo.com**) to download selected information from the Internet.

There are many other online resources available to us for staying current as lifelong learners. I am particularly a fan of resources that let you create customized versions of newspapers or magazines, including only the sections you are interested in. But getting the information is one thing—storing it, indexing it, and retrieving it later when you need it is a real challenge in this age of information overload. My personal recommendation is to find a good Personal Information Manager (PIM) and store your valuable nuggets in it. I like to use Microsoft Outlook with a synchronization strategy to allow it to stay current with a palm-sized device.

However you go about creating your knowledge management strategy, the key is that you come up with a plan that works for you, and that you get started on it now.

PART 2

NAVIGATING ORGANIZATIONAL CHANGE

▼

OVERVIEW

Change was once a *factor* of the business environment. Today, it *is* the environment. The first section of this book focused on how you can effectively manage change on a personal basis. As a leader who is on the forefront of change on a daily basis, chances are that many of the principles covered in that section hit close to home for you.

This section builds on those principles while focusing on the challenges of managing change in your organization. This discussion includes changes inflicted from the outside that you have little to no control over (e.g. economy, regulations, and climate), as well as those which you initiate yourself (usually as a response to external factors). Though the emphasis of this section is primarily on changes you initiate, look for broad application for change of all types in your organization.

LET'S REDEFINE THE METAPHOR

My use of the sailing metaphor is modified slightly for this section:
    You are still the *skipper*, but more so in the sense of your role as

a leader in your organization. You are the person responsible for making the journey successful.

The *crew* on your boat represents your staff—those people for whom you are responsible in your organization. It must be understood that the *boat* of this metaphor cannot be successfully sailed solo. The *skipper* is dependent on the *crew* to actually make progress.

The *journey* in this metaphor can represent a number of ongoing things—an initiative or a project, the aspects of your particular role, or the life of the company.

The *destination* and *horizon* represent your group's long-term mission and objectives—*where*, and in a sense, *why* you are journeying at all. In some settings, "long-term" might be just for the next year, or it might mean a longer duration.

The *wind* and *waves* represent changes that confront us on a daily basis. These are usually changes outside our control, but they can be caused by us *rocking the boat*!

Magnetic North and the *North Star* represent values which your organization deems deeply important. These are not changeless, but they tend to stay the same throughout your journey.

The *rudder*, *sails*, and *instruments* remain the tools we have at our disposal to interpret, respond to, and initiate change. Generally, these are things we have direct control over.

The term *organization* in this section can be defined as everything from a small team to an entire corporation. Consider *organization* to indicate you and your *crew*.

TOOLS FOR SKIPPERING ORGANIZATIONAL CHANGE

This section talks a lot about *change initiatives*. These could encompass many different things, including a reorganization or downsizing program, rolling out a new process or technology; new compensation, evaluation, or bonus programs; or a new mission or strategy.

Can you think of a change you are trying to make at your workplace right now? In order to give this section relevance, please keep that particular change in mind and apply the principles directly to it.

CHAPTER SIXTEEN

Plan to Succeed

▼

MOST EVERYONE IS FAMILIAR with the maxim, "Failure to plan is planning to fail." Yet change initiatives often fail for two equally fatal reasons related to planning: *too little* and *too much*. The *too little* often involves a failure to understand key roadblocks that could have been avoided with more forethought. It only takes a few years of managing to learn that one can never underestimate the ability of people to misinterpret our intentions. "Change plans" are often accompanied by sketchy communication, meaning that the troops never buy-in, which leaves the initiative dying on the vine.

The *too much* is less a problem for change initiatives in my experience. The problem here, though, is the unknowns. There are often just too many of them. By the time the most thorough of plans are delivered in mountains of documents, the playing field may have already changed significantly.

We've all known projects that suffered from either seat-of-the-pants management or *analysis/paralysis*. The *too much/too little* tension is a constant challenge for change leaders. To help guide you towards balanced planning, here are some areas for your consideration.

REMEMBER THE DYNAMICS OF PERSONAL CHANGE

Organizational change boils down to personal change for a group of individuals. Though such a statement might seem self-evident, many change initiatives start rocking the boat without appearing to take the individual into consideration. We might hear how the change will benefit the company, the stockholders, or the customers, but the average employee on the floor can be left wondering what it all means to him or her personally. Throw enough change at the staff and you can be left with an organization stuck at the *fall-behind point*. The issues discussed in the first section of this book are crucial for you to understand before planning and executing a change initiative at work.

DEFINE THE OBJECTIVES

Every change initiative needs to have clearly defined objectives. The entire leadership team must be sure of what the desired results are, why those results are important, and how those results will be measured. If management is not on board, your hope at convincing the rest of the crew is not founded.

If management is not on board, your hope at convincing the rest of the crew is not founded.

Whatever objectives you develop, here's a good exercise for you: *Put your objectives up against the organization's mission statement.* If the change affects a smaller group within the company, compare it against the mission you have for your department or even your team.

This, of course, implies there is such a mission statement, which is not a good assumption. Oh, there might be a one-page mission statement in the employee handbook or a lacquered plaque on the wall in the reception area, but that still doesn't count as a mission statement in my book. At least not yet. Here's a test for your organization's mission statement:

If you were asked to articulate the mission, could you (without just guessing)?

How many times in an average week do you make reference to your company's mission?

Can you honestly say your company's mission has been absorbed into the company's culture, such that employees honor it without even thinking about it?

The July 31, 1995, issue of *Advertising Age* had an interview with William Lynch, CEO of Leo Burnett. It was a great example of a company using a mission statement correctly. Mr. Lynch referred to the company mission, values, and principles more than five times in the relatively short article. He showed how it helped the leadership decide what businesses to work with, in what directions to head in the future, and how the company measures success on a daily basis.

Leo Burnett's culture has transcended its namesake. Notes the article: "Charisma is mortal, but a commitment to a core ideology can be passed on. It can not only guide the founding visionary to his wisdom; it can bequeath systems that will guide successors to wisdom in perpetuity."[11] In English, I read that to say that a mission statement, or core ideology, can be your *North Star* for navigating lasting change.

In summary, there are two primary points in this discussion on objectives thus far: have clearly defined objectives for your change initiative, and make sure those objectives line up with your organization's mission.

Before we move on to the next point, I want to give you a heads-up on a tension that often arises in change initiatives with respect to objectives. Peter Senge's *Fifth Discipline Fieldbook* calls it "the core dilemma." Here is how he describes it:

> *Inevitably, one of the factors that makes significant change difficult is conflict among competing goals and norms: we want to distribute power and authority and yet we also want to improve control and coordination. We want organizations to be more responsive to changes in their environment and yet more stable and coherent in their sense of identity, purpose, and vision. We want high productivity and high creativity. Good strategic thinking brings such dilemmas to the surface, and uses them to catalyze imagination and innovation.*[12]

My summary: Realize upfront that such dilemmas are part of the journey. Try to navigate them by setting good priorities, but realize they are generally inevitable.

UNDERSTAND THE "UNWRITTEN RULES"

There are always written and unwritten rules. In boating, there are detailed rules of the sea outlining who has the right of way under various situations. Such written rules have obvious value, but there are some almost universally understood *unwritten* rules that override the published ones, such as, "The biggest vessel gets the right-of-way." I'm not aware of too many small-boat skippers who spend much time pondering who has the right of way when the other vessel is an oil tanker! It's just understood.

Every organization has both written and unwritten rules. Unwritten rules are based on a collective mindset map that may or may not be anchored in reality (remember, mindset maps are only a representation of perceived reality). Think about your organization for a moment. What are the real motivators, written or unwritten? Who is more highly rewarded: the person who works weekends and all-nighters to finish a project (perhaps haphazardly), or the person who takes a little longer but whose finished work is normally bullet-proof? What is more highly prized by your senior management: delivering according to a date with little concern to quality, or delivering with high quality even if it means missing a deadline? Who is more likely to succeed in your organization: the person who never utters a word of bad news, or the person who says the truth regardless of how it will be received? Based on these few examples, take a moment to jot down some unwritten rules that exist in your organization (or consider doing this as an exercise with your team):

_____

_____

_____

_____

_____

LIMITING RESISTANCE

Though the written rules are certainly important, the critical factors in the failure of a change initiative can often be tied back to an issue with the unwritten rules. Here are some ideas for dealing with them:

Make sure you understand them. Start by looking closely at what the true motivators are for people in your organization. Find out who in the organization has a lot of sway, regardless of their location on the organizational chart. The *grapevine* is a great place to find unwritten rules. Leverage as many unwritten rules as you can to your advantage when it comes time to roll out your change initiative.

For rules that will resist your initiative, plan in advance how you will deal with them. Try to neutralize them by showing how your change addresses the underlying issue behind them. Consider emphasizing responses to the rules in your communications about the transition. Consistently reinforce the *new rules*. Whatever route you choose, do not ignore them, for they could be instrumental in keeping your initiative from being *dead on arrival*.

When you rock the boat with new things, it is inevitable that you will threaten the customs and comfort of some corners of the organization. Understanding the unwritten rules can help you through this challenge. For more information on this topic, I highly recommend the book *Understanding the Unwritten Rules of the Game* by Peter Scott-Morgan.

CHAPTER SEVENTEEN

Driving and Restraining Forces

▼

BEFORE I TOOK A CLASS on sailing, I always thought sailboats were pushed by the force of the wind against the sails. As it turns out, there are many forces at work that make a sailboat skim the water. In fact, the sails work together to form an airfoil, which causes lift, which drives the boat in motion. The keel on the bottom of the boat restrains the lateral force of the lift, moving the boat forward. The *driving* and *restraining forces* of a sailboat's design work together to advance the boat.

Change theory has some similar dynamics.

Kurt Lewin is generally regarded as the father of change theory. He developed the first model of the change process in the 1940s, called *Force Field Analysis*.[13] Essentially, Lewin's theory was that a current situation is defined by the relative strength of *driving forces* (those factors or pressures that strongly support change) and *restraining forces* (those factors or pressures which are obstacles to change). Lewin's term for the dynamic balance of forces was *quasi-stationary equilibrium* (or *Q-S equilibrium*). For change to occur, the Q-S equilibrium has to be altered by strengthening or adding driving forces, removing or reducing restraining forces, or varying the direction of some of the forces. Lewin's model sees behavior change through three phases:

unfreezing behavior, movement between positions, and refreezing behavior. Unfreezing requires sufficient dissatisfaction with the current method to try something new. After the movement occurs, refreezing is the phase where sufficient positive reinforcements (such as rewards, encouragement, compliments, etc.) cause the behavior to be adopted (a new mindset map).

With Lewin's theory in mind, you might find the following exercise helpful in your planning for a change initiative in your organization. Take a moment to consider what the potential driving and restraining forces are with respect to the change you are planning.

What are some driving forces that support the changes we want to make?

What actions can we take to strengthen those driving forces?

What are some restricting forces that could prevent the changes from being accepted?

What actions can we take to weaken or remove these restricting forces?

Important point: You need to closely scrutinize reward systems. Are your reward systems providing the necessary incentive to help implement lasting change? Here's an example: ACNielsen decided that employee satisfaction was going to be a fundamental area of focus within their organization. The senior management believed in a concept called the Service Profit Chain, which essentially says that higher employee satisfaction will lead to increased customer satisfaction, which eventually improves shareholder value. Though most people would agree that employee satisfaction is a good idea, there's a big difference between saying it and actually making it happen.

ACNielsen implemented a driving force of communicating the Service Profit Chain concept throughout the organization. You could not be an employee of the company without understanding the idea. They then implemented a survey process that provided an annual snapshot of how satisfied the employees were. That alone would have had some benefit, but ACNielsen went further. They tied a sizeable portion of employees' bonuses to improvement in the survey results.

If a manager was going to decide that she didn't care about this satisfaction initiative, inevitably the results would be clear from the annual survey and she would pay for this decision in a reduced annual bonus.

Tying compensation or other positive consequences (eligibility for promotion, schedule flexibility, opportunity for training, etc.) to change initiatives is a powerful way to strengthen driving forces and reduce restraining forces. Be creative with the reward systems and you will make a difference in effecting lasting change.

EVALUATE HOW READY THE CREW IS FOR CHANGE

There are better and worse times to launch changes. As part of your change planning, consider the following questions:

Is your crew already at the fall-behind point?

How dissatisfied are the people who are going to be most affected by the change? It is significantly easier to make a change when people are already dissatisfied.

If you don't think there is much dissatisfaction currently, can you create some dissatisfaction by highlighting areas in need of change?

Most organizations will never be completely ready for change, so don't sit back and wait for perfect conditions. The point of this section is to encourage you to spend some time in your planning to determine to what degree the organization is ready for more change before blindly rocking the boat with your initiative.

By intentionally analyzing the driving and restraining forces that are at work, you can better understand how to navigate through the change you want to lead. As you roll out the change-initiative, make it a point to re-analyze the forces to see if you are strengthening the driving ones and weakening the restraining ones. Adjust accordingly, and your opportunity to more effectively stay on course will increase dramatically.

CHAPTER EIGHTEEN

Communicating for Effective Change

By trying to crack down on resistance,
we do not neutralize it—
we just send it underground.

ANDY KAUFMAN

PERHAPS OUR BIGGEST FAILURE as leaders of change is that we all too often do not adequately and effectively communicate. How many times have you heard: "Management doesn't tell us anything," or "Management thinks too short-term," or "I would just like to know what's going on"? One of the best steps we can take to help people cope in times of high change is to communicate effectively. In these situations, it's better to be known as an over-communicator rather than a mystery. Here are some ideas for developing a powerful communication plan for your change initiative.

KEEP THEIR EYES ON THE HORIZON

Strive to keep the big picture relevant in all communications about the change. This has at least two benefits: 1) It forces *you* to keep your focus on the big picture as well, and 2) it helps provide employees a context for how this change fits into the grand scheme. *Context = Perspective*, which, as we learned earlier, is the formula for successfully dealing with change.

One practical way to do this in presentations is through the use of *decade slides*—slides often found at the beginning of presentations that show "where we have come from," "where we are," and "where we are going." Showing the big picture can help employees gain more of a *journey mindset*, making the turbulent change period easier to deal with because they know the reasons for it.

ALWAYS REMEMBER TO ARTICULATE THE "WHAT'S IN IT FOR ME" (WIIFM) AND THE "WHAT'S IN IT FOR US" (WIIFU)

When you announce the change, one of the primary things your crew will be trying to figure out is, "What's in it for me?" If you don't make it clear to people what's in it for them, they will come up with their own ideas, and generally people tend to focus on worst-case scenarios. Lack of clear *WIIFM* is the birth of resistance. We need to remember that resistance is really self-defense—a natural reaction to a perceived action that is not in a person's self-interest. Every time you write a memo or e-mail to your staff, give a presentation, or interact with customers, remember that what they really want to know is *WIIFM*. "What's in it for us" is acceptable too, as long as individuals can easily see themselves in the *us*. Even if "what's in it" isn't all that great, the risk of not articulating it is that your crew is likely to assume much worse.

BE SPECIFIC AND CONTINUOUS

Realize that a shout from the skipper does not cut it anymore. The case for change must be stated, reinforced, and absorbed into every corner of the organization. This takes time, patience, and often, thick skin. Once again, be guilty of over-communicating.

Asking our people for timeframe estimates and then expecting them to deliver on them is standard practice for managers. But too often we do not see upper management telling us *when* they will know more and then *delivering* on the "more." Accountability goes both ways. When communicating to your crew, be as specific as possible regarding timeframes, outcomes, and potential benefits. Then be sure to deliver on your promises.

BE HONEST

In the midst of a storm, people can see the storm clouds and the high waves. Don't try to tell people that everything's fine when it isn't. Honestly communicate as much as possible, as soon as possible.

The Price Waterhouse Change Integration Team wrote a volume called *Better Change*. A quote from that book is quite relevant here: "The first step in any change effort is to confront reality"—something which, according to them—"requires truth-telling." In Michael Silva and Terry McGann's book *Overdrive*, they say that when it comes to communicating good and bad news, "Choose substance over spin."

MAINTAIN "RICH" DIALOGUE

E-mail, memos, and voicemail can effectively be used (or abused) today. However, if you want to truly be an exceptional change leader, err on the side of the richest medium for the situation. For example, issues that are extremely sensitive and have great opportunity to be misunderstood require a richer medium—one which allows people to not only hear what you are saying but also to hear your tone and see your face and body language. Issues of less significance to an organization, such as a minor change to a relatively unimportant policy, do not require as rich a medium. In that case, a memo or e-mail would probably suffice.

The richest medium available is face-to-face communication, whether one-on-one or in front of groups of people. Face-to-face can be increasingly challenging with virtual teams distributed geographically. Regardless, one of the keys is to allow people to express concerns and frustrations, and ask the tough questions. The pressure must be allowed to escape, and this is often best done through real, honest dialogue using the richest and most appropriate medium available.

William O'Brien, former CEO of the Hanover Insurance Company emphasizes that a key to leading change in today's business world is:

conversation. . . . This is the single greatest learning tool in your organization—more important than computers or sophisticated research. . . . When we face contentious issues—when there are feelings about rights, or when two worthwhile principles come in conflict with one another—we have so many defense mechanisms that impede communications that we are absolutely terrible. To navigate this enormous change we're going through, a corporation must become good at conversation that isn't polite.[14]

When was the last time you were encouraged to have impolite conversations at work? I have a firm conviction that we must make it safe for employees to express resistance. By trying to crack down on resistance, we do not neutralize it—we just send it underground. Seek to create situations for dialogue.

GET ALL HANDS ON DECK

There must be acknowledgment from the beginning that true, lasting change fundamentally requires buy-in from all hands on deck. This means that the people up and down the ladder support the changes that are being rolled out. Though this is a requirement for lasting change, getting this buy-in can be quite tricky.

A successful technique for engaging people in a change is to include them in the planning and design sessions. Stephen Covey is on record with this principle: "No involvement, no commitment." "Involving" people in this context has to do with sharing the responsibilities, the challenges, the problems, and the rewards. It means not shoving down initiatives from on high, but building them throughout the organization. Ownership of the problem/change needs to seep as deep into the organization as possible. If not, people who do not own at least a part of the problem will be dragging anchors at best and torpedoes at worst.

Giving people ownership of problems might require releasing control that has been dearly held on to in the past. O'Brien continues: "The forthcoming kind of company is going to require voluntary followership. Most of our leaders don't think in terms of getting voluntary followers; they think in terms of control." Releasing some control is a key to getting all hands on deck and wrestling with the same issue instead of throwing rocks at it (and the people leading the change).

Here are some practical ideas on how you can work to get buy-in throughout your organization. These tips come from *Understanding Organizational Change*:

> *Involve employees in measurement/evaluation systems.*

> *Encourage different employees to conduct meetings.*

> *Know when to leave the room by recognizing when your presence is impeding progress.*

> *Involve employees in analyzing problems to establish ownership further into the organization.*[15]

The message must be clear: you cannot simply proclaim that you are going to be changing things and expect that people will automatically embrace it. However, by using ideas such as involving employees in the process, aligning rewards systems, and clearly communicating why the changes are being made (along with anticipated benefits), you will make great progress toward creating lasting change in your organization.

CHAPTER NINETEEN

Are We
Making Progress?

▼

ON ONE OF MY FIRST SAILING OUTINGS, I learned the
meaning of the term "*course made good.*" After sailing for hours with
the wind in our faces, we were far enough offshore that it wasn't
clear exactly where we were just by sight. The crew had been
absorbed in personal conversations enough not to have paid attention to the map.

After a while we all took guesses on our progress. Then we used
the navigation systems on board to see who was closest. It turned
out that we were all way off! The wind in our faces had made it
feel like we were going much faster than we were. Our progress—
what sailors call Course Made Good—had been much less than
we'd thought.

In times of rapid change, we must constantly evaluate our
group's *course made good.* The best way to do so is by comparing it
with something fixed or immovable—something which is not my
winds and waves, like our group's mission, objectives, and goals. By
reviewing progress, we might find aspects of our goals that need to
be revised. Perhaps we need to make some course corrections to
achieve unchanged goals. Slight course variations for short periods
of time are not generally a problem as long as they are compensated
for with minor course adjustments.

WATCH FOR PITFALLS

Regardless of how well you plan, things will go wrong. Among pitfalls to watch for are these, according to the Price Waterhouse team:

> *You fail to deliver early, tangible results.* (Come up with early wins—don't rely on the "big bang" at the end.)

> *You talk about breakthroughs while drowning in detail.* (Breakthroughs are often achieved by simplifying rather than complicating. Don't drown potential breakthroughs in meticulous documentation and long meetings.)

> *You treat everything as a high priority.* (Make choices.)

> *Old performance measures block change.* (Root them out— these are related to Written/Unwritten Rules.)

> *The voice of the customer is absent.* (Systematically assess what the customer wants and trumpet the results.)

> *The voice of the employee is absent.* (Might be messy, but necessary.)

> *You haven't made "What's in it for me?" clear to everyone.*

> *Same old horses, same old glue.* (Team filled with status quo types, not innovators.)[16]

FOCUS

Focus requires us to constantly review our priorities. It must be assumed that the "plan" will change. The issue is making sure we stay focused on the essential priorities at each windshift. We must also continually focus people on the big picture as each change hits. The "What's in it for me?" and "What's in it for us?" must be absolutely clear to everyone.

CHAPTER TWENTY

Create a
Change Culture

▼

CREATING A CULTURE in your organization where change is expected and dealt with responsibly has enormous benefits. The old phrase, "An ounce of prevention is worth a pound of cure," is relevant in this regard. By proactively shaping and maintaining a flexible environment, you can minimize resistance to change down the road.

With that in mind, it is important to go into this discussion with proper expectations. Building a culture of any kind in a company takes time. Organizational dynamics are not created overnight. They are not solely established with posters on walls, dress-code revisions, or management directives. Cultures are built a day at a time and a person at a time. Massive mindset re-mapping might very well be necessary, so set your expectations correctly, and then get started!

YOUR CREW—YOUR MOST VALUABLE ASSET

The most valuable asset of your organization is the people. Peter Drucker has been saying for years that knowledge is "the only meaningful economic resource." When your top performer walks out of your office, you have an inestimable amount of knowledge walking out as well. Of course, the goal will never be to retain all people at all costs. However, you cannot afford to have them walk for all the wrong reasons.

In the *Small Business Management Guide*, author Jim Schell talks about how "customers aren't everything; employees are everything."

In their book, *The Service Profit Chain: How Leading Companies Link Profit and Growth to Loyalty, Satisfaction, and Value*, authors Heskett, Sasser, and Schlesinger reinforce the importance of the employees. They assert that we should first focus on employee satisfaction. Why? It goes like this: Highly satisfied employees have a better likelihood of nurturing highly satisfied customers, and money will inevitably flow from very satisfied customers.[17] In an environment where the focus seems first on the money and last on the employees, perhaps this formula is most needed today.

Does the formula make sense to you? Are satisfied salespeople more likely to better serve their customers? Are satisfied ministry staff better able to take care of their flock? Are satisfied teachers likely to more effectively pour into their students? The Service Profit Chain concept says, "Yes!"

Part of building a team of stars is looking for people who embrace change. Resistance impedes growth and destroys opportunities. Schell recommends trying to assess "change hardiness" during initial interviews to help build a culture of change. Once you have the crew built, make sure they never forget that you value them as the most prized asset of the company.

DIVERSITY IN OPINION

When I was a new manager, I looked forward to the day when my crew quickly and unanimously agreed with everything I said—and with each other. Such quick consensus-building was my goal. Over the years, however, I have learned there is wisdom in not rushing to consensus. Quick consensus can often leave better ideas and solutions unsurfaced. In addition, it might be a sign that employees are not engaged enough in the decision-making process. *Why work to come up with additional solutions when the boss is just going to do what she wants anyway?* If you are to create a culture that can respond effectively to change throughout the journey, learn to welcome and encourage divergent opinions.

If you think consensus is being reached too quickly in your group, here's a practical tip: Designate a "devil's advocate" in meetings. Give one person this specific role through an entire meeting, freeing him or her to jump in and bring up divergent opinions. Once you do this a couple of times, people will start catching on that varying ideas are encouraged (without having to *walk the plank* afterwards!).

The sign of a good team is when you can have diversity in opinions, yet unity in decisions. Everyone gets their say, but they walk out supporting whatever is decided. This dynamic takes time, good leadership, and a culture that rewards this behavior.

COMMITMENT TO LEARNING

We have already talked about the need to establish a personal commitment to lifelong learning. Such a commitment is necessary to stay on course. The same is true for your organization. There must be a mindset within your teams that lifelong learning is a fundamental part of the culture. This includes the normal skill-training that our people would expect. But it also includes training in some of the *softer skill* areas as well, like time management, leading change, and conflict resolution.

The issue is much broader than simply making sure your people get enough hours of training in classrooms and seminars. It gets down to truly growing your staff and helping them, in effect, to learn how to learn. This means putting them into situations where they have to assume new responsibilities and develop new ways of doing things. It means repeatedly asking the question, "What did we learn from this?" It means challenging ourselves and our people to not leave the office on Friday without being able to say, "I learned something new this week."

This culture of lifelong learning in an organization is not simply to keep people happy. In *The Fifth Discipline Fieldbook*, William O'Brien states that success comes down to our ability to marry together "individual growth and economic performance. You can never separate them. If you are to walk down one road without the other, you will not build a great organization."[18]

The training model for many teams consists of employees randomly requesting permission to attend a class (that may or may not be related to their objectives). If workload and company budgets allow, it is usually approved. This random approach can yield some benefit, but there are many employees who are not investing that training time as effectively as they could, and others who just don't proactively request to go to classes at all.

You know you have started on the path towards being a learning organization when managers and employees sit down and talk about training goals and then execute a training plan during the year. You know you are getting somewhere when a project is not allowed to end without a retrospective being conducted to review what was learned.

FOLLOW-THROUGH

As with most things in life, it's easier to start something than to finish it. Change initiatives are certainly no different. If you demonstrate a track record of starting initiatives based on the latest "flavor of the month" technique without a commitment to following through on the programs, you will soon find yourself leading a cynical workforce that resists even the most sincere efforts. Follow-through needs to be part of your culture. Make commitments to your crew and then deliver on them. Treat promises to employees like you treat their promises on deadlines.

WATCHING THE RADAR

The future can be a fascinating, fearful, and sometimes entertaining topic to study. Though no one can expect to make all the calls correctly over time, it is important to force yourself to watch the horizon for new trends. This is certainly not an exercise for simple enjoyment—the stakes are too high. There are a myriad of methods you can use to scan the horizon, but it is important to pick a few and do them well. Here are some ideas:

Keep a pulse on the people who have the power to shape the

future. Anybody can call themselves a business guru, from the professor at a university to a psychic in the *National Enquirer!* As interesting as it may be to dream about the future, the key is to pay attention to the people who have the resources (e.g. funding, influence) to actually create the future.

Consider having periodic "forecast" sessions. In a forecast session, members of your team gather to discuss trends they feel are beginning to appear. These sessions can be guided by using questions like:

What new conditions are we facing that we didn't face a year ago? Five years ago?

Who are new potential competitors that have recently popped up?

What are some new products you've seen that have given you an idea for making us more efficient/helping us provide better value to our customers?

What do we need to do to be more competitive/deliver with higher quality?

Forecast sessions provide a number of direct benefits, including: detecting trends early, thus allowing a chance to take advantage of them; training team members in areas outside their typical circles of knowledge; and helping team members look beyond their current problems. We need excuses to look past our present circumstances, and forecast sessions can do just that.

COMMITMENT FOR THE LONG HAUL

Successful change management cannot be measured through a simple short-term analysis. True "change success" is measured in the long-term. If you are aiming to build an organizational culture that thrives on change, remember to balance your expectations and goals between short-term wins and long-term victories.

SOME
FINAL THOUGHTS
▼

THROUGHOUT THESE PAGES we have discussed a number of concepts, tools, and techniques that have proven to be helpful in managing personal and organizational change. We have learned that the key issue in dealing with change effectively is perspective. In the process of working to gain better perspective, we have talked about taking on a journey mindset, which keeps an eye on the horizon while dealing with the winds and the waves of today. From mission statements to mindset maps, from unmet needs to unwritten rules, we have covered a boatload of ideas that are yours for the taking to start applying in your life.

A CALL TO ACTION

If perspective was an easy thing to achieve, our turbulent journey would just be another outing. But that's not the case. At the beginning of this book, you were challenged to look for at least one lesson, tool, or tip that you can start implementing in your life now. Did you find it? Now is the time to take it from the pages of a book to the story of your life.

Over the years I have found that the process of trying to implement new lessons or tools in my life is a bit like New Year's resolutions: good intentions in January, trouble following through in February, and out of the picture by March. Good intentions are important, but they are just that—intentions. I would like to challenge you to seek more than good intentions for the change you have identified. Here's how:

Take a moment to commit in writing the changes you plan on making as a result of the insight you've gained from this book. Use the space below. Make sure to note the following:

What are you going to change or implement?

Why do you want to do this?

What steps do you need to take to accomplish this change?

What obstacles do you foresee that must be expected and prepared for?

What resources will you need to make this happen?

How will you deal with setbacks?

How will you reward yourself for succeeding?

This is a lot of detail to think through, but experience has shown that the more we consider these questions, the more likely we are to really change.

Tell at least one other person about this. Ask them to keep you accountable by regularly checking up to see how you are progressing.

Pull out your calendar now and schedule in the time you need to get started.

Finally, once you have decided to make a commitment to change, send me an e-mail (**andy@i-leadonline.com**) to tell me about it! It would certainly encourage me to hear about your plans and how you are progressing.

Thomas Aquinas observed: "If the primary mission of a captain were to preserve his ship, he would never leave port." Though the peace of the port would certainly be a nice option every once in a while, the thrill in life—the place where the defining moments of our lives are penned—is out on the high seas. This time of high change is filled with opportunity for those who are willing to turn into the wind and learn how to harness the turbulent forces. By investing the time to read this book and facing up to the challenges presented here, you are taking a great step towards seizing the opportunity that is yours for the taking. Both in your personal and professional life, I wish you great success as you seek to stay on course and navigate the winds of change!

ACKNOWLEDGMENTS

MY JOURNEY THUS FAR IN LIFE has been greatly influenced by more people than I could possibly name here. However, I want to take the opportunity of my first book to recognize many of the trustworthy members of my crew, some of whom have traveled with me for many legs of the journey, others of whom have just recently blessed my life.

I cannot imagine being on this journey without my wife Sara. Your encouragement, wisdom, support, and godly commitment to being a faithful life partner are an inspiration to me. Your fingerprints are on everything I do. You are the exclamation point of my life.

Being the father of Barrett, Zachary, and Christa has taught me so much about the journey of life. May your journeys take you to destinations beyond your wildest dreams, and may you be godly influences for good on each leg along the way.

Thank you to Bill and Karen Kaufman for the sacrifices you made to bring me into this world and to raise Kaylene, Mary, Cindy, and me. Thank you for the love I have always known through the years.

This book would not have been possible without the expert guidance of Kris Bearss. Your years of friendship to our family are greatly cherished. Thank you for assembling the dream team of Bearss, Kiple, and DeBoer! May you all be richly blessed for your generous gift of involvement in this project.

My love for sailing and the discovery of the parallels to life have been fueled by annual sailing adventures with John Chmela (www.chmela.com) and Jim Ritchhart. You both have had a unique influence on me, and I have great respect and deep admiration for the ways you seek to fulfill your personal missions in life.

My life has been enriched by the teaching and example of Dr. James MacDonald (www.walkintheword.com). Your passion for clearly communicating and leading the body at Harvest Bible Chapel (www.harvestbible.org) has been a living example for me and has greatly influenced my own communication style. Also from Harvest I would like to acknowledge the influence that Jim Jodrey, Rick Donald, Mel Svendsen (www.hbcvh.org), Joe Stowell, Joe Mirigala, and Hal Rich have had on me personally and professionally.

I have had the privilege of learning from many talented leaders over the years, including Jim Heineger, Diane Conrath, Mark Pietscher, Walt Wikman, Bill Brennan, Ken Bridgeman, Bill Henry, Bill Nold, Bernie Ostrowsky, and Cindy Elzinga. Each taught me and stretched me in a way that has indelibly marked my leadership style.

Special thanks to Stan Piskorski and the friends at Windy City Professional Speakers (www.geocities.com/windycitytm) and the Toastmasters Club at Motorola in Schaumburg for helping raise the bar for my presentations. In addition, a special thank you to Laurie Guest (www.laurietalk.com), Karl Wiegers (www.processimpact.com), Carolyn Thompson (www.trainingsys.com), and Johanna Rothman (www.jrothman.com) for consistently welcoming my questions on how to build a business that effectively helps people learn.

In 1981, George Taylor introduced me to the one person who has been my greatest help in navigating change and staying on course.

Through challenging storms and peaceful days, the key factor that separates who I am today from who I was before is Jesus. There is immeasurable power in basing your life on the One who said He is "the same yesterday, today, and tomorrow." In a world of constant change, Jesus Christ has been my Rock. If there is any question, may it be known today that He is the source of my energy, enthusiasm, and any good that comes from the steps I take each day.

NOTES

[1]Falkland, Lord Lucius Cary (1610-43), English statesman, soldier, patron.

[2]Hanks, Kurt. *The Change Navigator* (Menlo Park, CA: Crisp Publications, 1992).

[3]Swindoll, Charles R. *Strengthening Your Grip* (Dallas, TX: Word, Inc., 1982).

[4]Carnegie, Dale. *How to Stop Worrying and Start Living* (New York: Simon and Schuster, 1948), p. 13.

[5]Covey, Merrill, and Merrill. *First Things First* (New York: Simon and Schuster, 1994), p. 110.

[6]This list, as well as much of the content for the discussion on mindset maps, has been influenced by Kurt Hanks' work in *The Change Navigator*.

[7]Hanks, pp. 131-132.

[8]Hedges, Newman, and Cary. "What's Wrong with the FAA?" *U.S. News & World Report*, June 26, 1995.

[9]Covey, Merrill, and Merrill, p. 45.

[10]O'Connell, Vanessa. "Boosting Your Earnings in an Uncertain World," *The Wall Street Journal*, Friday, February 9, 1996, C1.

[11]McDonough. "Burnett—An Enduring Culture," *Advertising Age,* July 31, 1995, LB-2.

[12]Senge, Peter, et al. *The Fifth Discipline Fieldbook* (New York: Doubleday, 1994), p. 17.

[13]The material on Kurt Lewin's Force Field Analysis is from Lynn Fossum's *Understanding Organizational Change* (Menlo Park, CA: Crisp Publications, 1989), pp. 13-16.

[14]Senge, et al, p. 14.

[15]Fossum, p. 67.

[16]Price Waterhouse Change Integration Team. *Better Change* (McGraw-Hill Professional Publishing, 1994).

[17]Heskett, Sasser, Schlesinger. *The Service Profit Chain: How Leading Companies Link Profit and Growth to Loyalty, Satisfaction, and Value.* (New York: Free Press, April 1997).

[18]Senge, et al, p. 15.